NATO:
Issues and Prospects

Contemporary Affairs No. 38

NATO:
Issues and Prospects

Harald von Riekhoff

The Canadian Institute of International Affairs
230 Bloor Street West, Toronto, Ontario

Printed and Bound in Canada
by
John Deyell Limited/Lindsay/Ontario

Table of Contents

Preface

The North Atlantic Alliance remains one of the most closely observed and most carefully documented subjects in current international relations. In turning to the subject again, even at the risk of being somewhat eclectic and of lacking a central theme, this short work tries to examine those features and problems of the Atlantic Alliance that have not formed the focus of analysis or that should be reconsidered in the light of recent changes.

Since NATO involves political questions of considerable current concern, the subject has quite naturally attracted the kind of analysis that may be referred to as problem-solving. But by taking this particular approach, analysts tend to treat all Alliance problems in terms of specific policy issues, without giving sufficient emphasis to those questions that arise from NATO's basic structure and from the inherent limitations of alliances in the nuclear age. Another aspect of NATO that deserves a more substantial treatment than it has received is the role of the smaller powers within the Alliance—their contributions, influence, and attitudes.

The last few years have witnessed a marked acceleration in the pace of political change in Europe. Only a few years ago, NATO analysts tended to look for a kind of carefully planned and centrally controlled process of political transformation in Europe that would involve a supranational European Community and a North American one, if not also a politically integrated Atlantic structure that would bargain for changes in the *status quo* by holding formal negotiations with the Warsaw Pact powers.

At present we are probably more inclined to dismiss such orderly slide-rule techniques. The centrifugal political effects of the super-power strategic equilibrium and partial East-West *détente* are more likely to produce changes that are sporadic rather than planned, that stem from unilateral or bilateral actions and not from multilateral measures, and that come into being by way of example and influence rather than by formal treaty negotiations.

If the political horoscope for Europe indicates change, this does not necessarily guarantee a carefully guided and centrally controlled process. In an area as highly interdependent and as vulnerable as Europe, a major transformation of political forces entails serious risks of conflict or reaction, if it proceeds without central guidance and co-ordination. Since supranational community structures are not likely to be available to pilot this major project through its dangerous course, we have to look for other stabilizing sources. This study seeks to inquire whether there is a role for an institution like NATO, which relies on common planning and policy co-ordination rather than on more ambitious forms of supranationalism, in facilitating the emergence of a new order in Europe.

This study is the outcome of a defence research fellowship that was jointly sponsored by the Canadian Institute of International Affairs and the School of International Affairs of Carleton University. I am grateful to both institutions for the award and for an additional grant that made it possible for me to spend some time at NATO headquarters in Paris, as well as in London and Bonn. In January 1966 the School and the Institute also jointly sponsored a conference at Carleton University on the question of NATO's future. The views and comments of the conference participants, many of whom had considerable experience in NATO matters, provided an excellent cross-section of informed Canadian opinion and were very helpful to me in the final stages of the study.

While I must bear full responsibility for the final outcome, I am truly indebted to a great number of persons who have given me their advice and criticism. I am particularly grateful to Mr. John W. Holmes, Director General of the Canadian Institute of International Affairs, and to Professors Norman A. Robertson, Robert A. MacKay, and Peyton V. Lyon of the School of International Affairs of Carleton University.

All of these as well as the late Dr. Robert J. Sutherland and Mr. Jack Trotman of the Department of National Defence and General Charles Foulkes kindly read the manuscript and offered many helpful suggestions.

Special thanks go to Mr. George Ignatieff, Canadian Ambassador to the UN and formerly Ambassador to NATO, for allowing me to profit from his intimate knowledge of NATO affairs and the broad historical perspective of his views. Air Vice-Marshal R. A. Cameron and Colonel W. C. Leonard, then on the military staff of the Canadian delegation to the North Atlantic Council, and Air Marshal W. R. MacBrien and General Count Wolf von Baudissin of SHAPE enlightened me on many military points.

I benefited also from conversations with Mr. J. Roberts, Deputy Secretary General of NATO; Lord Chalfont, British Minister for Disarmament; the Hon. Alastair Buchan of the Institute for Strategic Studies; General André Beaufre of the Institut Français d'Etudes Stratégiques; Mr. Andrew Brewin, M.P.; Dr. Joachim Jaenicke, NATO's Assistant Secretary General for Political Affairs; Dr. Uwe Nerlich of the Forschungsinstitut der Deutschen Gesellschaft für Auswärtige Politik; Dr. Theo Sommer of *Die Zeit*; and Dr. Michael Sherman of the Hudson Institute. Professor Jon McLin of the University of Alabama kindly let me read the manuscript of his book on Canadian defence policy. Group Captain William Lee, Special Assistant to the Minister of

National Defence, made arrangements for my visit to Canadian Forces in Metz and Soest.

I have had a long series of enjoyable and profitable talks with many officers of the Department of External Affairs, the Department of National Defence, and the German Auswärtige Amt who, by the golden rule of civil service anonymity, would prefer to remain unnamed.

Mrs. Joan Lloyd of the CIIA Library kindly made available her inexhaustible clipping files that revealed great treasures on NATO history. My research assistant, Douglas Rosenthal, provided many useful services and during my numerous periods of absence acted as a steady link with Ottawa. I would also like to thank Mrs. Pearl Fisher, Mrs. Mary Jones, and Miss Carol Benway, all on the secretarial staff of the Carleton Political Science Department, for having cheerfully and efficiently coped with the many variations of the manuscript; Scotland Yard could not enjoy a better deciphering section.

Ottawa   HARALD VON RIEKHOFF
July 1967

NATO:
Issues and Prospects

1
Alliance Beyond
the Regional Principle

POLICY-MAKERS AND ANALYSTS have naturally tended to concentrate their efforts on the more specific problems which confront the Atlantic Alliance at the close of the second decade of its existence. Foremost among these problems are such questions as allied nuclear sharing and control, crisis management and contingency planning, military integration and political partnership. Some of these specific items will be examined in subsequent chapters. In view of this very necessary preoccupation with specifics, it might be of use to examine some of the more fundamental problems of alliances in the nuclear age. Many of the items on the current list of unresolved Alliance problems may, indeed, be attributed to one country, one person, or one particular strategy. But to view them entirely in this manner and without reference to the wider context of coalition behaviour, not only provides us with a distorted and oversimplified version of reality, but also tends to foster the over-optimistic belief that a few specific remedial measures, like aspirin, can offer "quick and lasting relief".

Some of the difficulties now confronting the North At-

3

lantic Alliance are chronic coalition ailments from which alliances have suffered ever since the days of the Delian League. The dilemma stems from the fact that consensus among a group of countries cannot but find its common denominator on a level that falls short of the particular interests of each participant, whose aim it is to have the efforts and purposes of the alliance coincide exactly with purely national aims and policies. Insofar as these multiple national policies cannot always be identical, alliances have had to sail the treacherous straits between the Scylla of trying to prevent clashes of interests between allies, at the expense of inactivity and a low level of common efforts, and the Charybdis of undertaking more extensive commitments in face of the danger that this might force the entire alliance into supporting the particular national aims of one or a few of the more powerful member states.

In NATO some of these chronic alliance deficiencies have become intensified because the wide region covered by the Alliance, the large number of participants, and the duration of the commitment generally exceed those of historical alliances.

While NATO profits from common experiences, practices, and institutions which have emerged as the result of nearly two decades of uninterrupted operation, this prolonged duration has imposed certain stresses on the workings of the Alliance. It becomes increasingly difficult to sustain major material efforts and strong emotional commitments over a protracted time period, all the more if there is no more direct way of measuring success than in the deterrence of an undesired, but in no way certain, eventuality.

Customarily alliances have operated on a regional basis. Only a very liberal interpretation would regard those countries which string the shores of the North Atlantic as a compact region, and even this definition could hardly accommodate such countries as Greece and Turkey. What has given an element of cohesion to this diverse collection of countries is less a feeling of geographical proximity than the consciousness of a common threat and of shared historical experiences and traditions and the belief in common values and institutions.

The cohesive influence of these symbolic factors was particularly pronounced during the creative period of common postwar reconstruction in the face of a massive external threat. However, now that reconstruction has been completed and the Soviet threat has diminished, thereby increasing the feeling of security and reducing the basis for emotional solidarity, a greater degree of national particularism in policy must be anticipated. The very evaluation of the threat now constitutes a matter of dispute between those who urge preparedness for every conceivable form of warfare and those who, like General de Gaulle, base their policy "on the thesis that there can be no war, certainly not a conventional one."[1] Disagreement on strategy may thus, in part at least, be regarded as a form of disagreement by proxy on more far-reaching issues.

The scattering of some 15 members over three continents not only poses problems in retaining a meaningful level of homogeneity and common interest, which is required for the sake of reaching consensus, but it poses a delicate strategic dilemma of imbalanced vulnerability. Allied cohesion would demand that allies assume an equitable share of defence burdens and risks. But the North American members, because of their geographic location and different distribution of population, are not as exposed as their European counterparts, despite the levelling influence of intercontinental missiles. During the massive retaliation phase the European allies were concerned lest the virtual invulnerability of the North American continent might prompt the United States to be too trigger-happy and thus liable to respond to a minor incident by initiating a nuclear war, the destructive effects of which would largely be suffered in Europe.

[1] Dirk Stikker, "The Role of the Secretary General of NATO", in Edgar Furniss, Jr., ed., *The Western Alliance* (Columbus: Ohio State University Press, 1965), p. 19. Mr. Stikker recounts his interview with General de Gaulle in 1961 during his tenure as Secretary General.

Now America's strategic vulnerability has reversed the dilemma. The European allies are less concerned with the premature use of nuclear weapons than with the problem of relying on the U.S., despite its vulnerable state, to resort to nuclear war in the defence of its NATO allies. Similarly, it was felt that the strategy of flexible response, which was subsequently designed by the United States, was too closely tailored to its own security needs. For while it exempted the United States from the necessity of immediately discharging its obligations by nuclear means, it exposed Europe to the full impact of modern conventional war and of tactical nuclear weapons, and to the risk of being over-run, none of which threatened the American continent. Certain critics of American alliance policy have gone so far as to equate the strategy of flexible response to an American nuclear disengagement from Europe.[2]

The preponderance of U.S. power over that of its allies, singly or collectively, constitutes another major difficulty in the North American Alliance. From the strictly military point of view this concentration of power in the hands of one nation, unimpeded by the requirement for multinational consent and unfettered by Allied veto rights, has been an asset in preserving the credibility of the deterrent. Initially the European allies accepted without demur this custodial responsibility by the United States. Not only did it constitute the only tolerable and reliable security arrangement available to them at that time, but in the postwar atmosphere of apathy and pessimism about their own capacity to form a viable political framework and workable security system, Europeans derived some sense of relief and comfort from this transfer of responsibility to a peripheral custodial power.

As the result of Europe's remarkable political, economic, and psychological recovery, such a unilateral custodial relationship no longer provides a satisfactory condition for a

[2] See Premier Georges Pompidou's address to the French National Assembly, April 20, 1966. Cited in the *New York Times*, April 21, 1966.

European partnership in NATO. As France's former Minister of Information, M. Alain Peyrefitte, expressed it, Europeans "must face up to the situation that no amount of 'multilateral' gimmickry can turn the clock back to the comfortable (for us) years of U.S. monopoly in nuclear weapons and decision-making within the alliance."[3] Even those European allies who are willing to accept continued U.S. leadership and custody over nuclear weapons are firm in their demand that Europeans be allowed to define their own interests and to join in the process of developing those strategies which are concerned with their own defence.

From the standpoint of maximizing cohesion within the Atlantic region, the geographical area covered by NATO exceeds optimum size. However, if viewed from a different perspective, the circumference of responsibilities may be too narrowly delineated. The contractual responsibilities of the Alliance are clearly defined with respect to area and there is no dispute that these are restricted to the immediate region of the Alliance. But this contractual certainty does not answer the question of strategic expediency. If one assumes that NATO serves the purpose of providing for the security of its members and accepts that the present form of aggression and subversion, Communist or otherwise, in areas outside the NATO region constitutes an indirect threat to Alliance members, the question arises whether NATO membership involves any responsibility for threats of this kind. Even a positive answer does not solve the question of whether such responsibility should find expression through consultation, through a declaration of moral support for those allies which are independently engaged in combatting threats of this kind, or through joint military assistance to non-NATO members.

Given the content of present-day interdependence in international relations, this poses an inevitable dilemma. The dilemma is heightened by the discrepancy of power within the Atlantic Alliance, insofar as the United States is not only NATO's major partner but also the only member

[3] *New York Times*, June 28, 1963.

with far-reaching global commitments. As NATO was initially conceived, it was designed to meet an overt military threat in a clearly delineated area. The problem of NATO's ultra-peripheral threats has been heightened by a growing awareness of global interdependence, by the proliferation of unilateral foreign commitments by the United States concomitant with the retreat of her principal European allies from those areas, and by the shifting emphasis in Communist strategy from a direct advance in Europe to global encirclement by more indirect and less drastic means.

Even if the European allies give their consent in principle to the necessity of halting Communist advances beyond the NATO periphery, in actual practice, as in the case of Viet Nam, there has been a notable reluctance to convert this agreement in principle into a more concrete commitment. American policy-makers, with righteous indignation, have pointed out that they have undertaken commitments for the sake of the free world rather than for purely national interests but that "the willingness to accept world responsibility—as distinct from the preservation of national interests —is . . . not universal among the NATO membership."[4] Americans have tried to explain this reluctance as part of the inexperience of European powers in assuming world responsibility "except in defense and support of world empire."[5]

The explanation seems more complex than that and must be found largely in psychological terms. Much of the

[4] Under-Secretary George Ball; cited in Karl Cerny and Henry Briefs, eds., *NATO in Quest of Cohesion* (New York: Praeger, 1965. Published for the Hoover Institution on War, Revolution, and Peace), p. 18. Not all allies will agree with Under-Secretary Ball's interpretation. See John W. Holmes's reply to Mr. Ball's speech: "I think it is essential for the United States to recognize that other countries are not merely acting in their own national interests. I do not know what on earth Canadian troops are doing in Cyprus, or why we have been in Indochina for ten years—unless it is perhaps assumed that we happen to be on the purer side of the Atlantic." Cited in *ibid.*, p. 109.

[5] George Ball, "The Dangers of Nostalgia", *Atlantic Community Quarterly*, III, No. 2 (Summer 1965), p. 172.

European aversion against renewed international commitments beyond their immediate home regions stems from the reluctance to make costly material investments in foreign engagements over which, in the face of U.S. preponderance, they could scarcely hope to exercise a more substantial control than from a position of total abstinence. Secondly, after the recent and frequently traumatic retreat from their former colonies, there exists little desire on the part of the Europeans to stage another re-engagement, now in the guise of peace-makers or freedom-fighters, other than in the economic sphere. Furthermore, those social classes and attitudes which were instrumental in supporting a foreign policy of imperialism no longer play a determining role in the political life of the European powers of today. Most important, however, these weaker and more vulnerable allies share an almost instinctive fear of engaging in any military effort other than that which is related to their immediate defence, lest such action provoke a counterstrike against their own territory, either as the consequence of direct retaliation or as the result of gradual escalation.[6] Rational arguments, to the effect that the best way of halting a possible Communist aggression in Europe is through meeting such aggression in other areas, offer little counterweight in the presence of such instinctive reservations.

Ironically, with respect to the NATO role in non-Atlantic regions the respective European and U.S. positions have

[6] If conflicts in the third world in which the United States was committed were to escalate, the enemy target would probably be U.S. forces or bases in that region or, at worst, a massive nuclear strike against the American continent rather than against American installations in the European region of NATO. However, Premier Pompidou in his above-mentioned speech to the French *Chambre* tried to justify French Alliance policy precisely in terms of the latter threat. "If one day there was a conflict between the United States and Russia over issues that have nothing to do with France and her obligations under the alliance, who can maintain that the presence of American headquarters, communications, air bases and depots would not constitute an obvious and serious risk for us. We could not be forced to declare war, I admit. But all this would turn us into a target for atomic bombs." Cited in the *New York Times*, April 21, 1966.

become reversed. During the early years of the Alliance the European colonial powers, and especially France, felt that their colonial military operations represented crusades of freedom against Communist encroachments and thus deserved the sympathy as well as the moral, and possibly even material, support of the other NATO allies. Despite these arguments, U.S. policy remained skeptical or at best equivocal toward the efforts of its European partners in preserving their imperial domains. In turn, the United States now finds itself with little sympathy and no direct support from its European allies in its engagement in Viet Nam, which it regards as a forward defence strategy for the Atlantic area.

In addition, various psychological cleavages torment the Alliance. The European members of NATO are heirs to a long tradition of membership in various alliances. This tradition includes, among others, a record of broken alliance commitments and faulty alliance management under far less critical conditions than those which may be anticipated in a future crisis. The present European suspicion about the future of the American guarantee, vexing and unfounded as this may appear to the chief guarantor, cannot be divorced from this historical experience. The United States, on the other hand, has become historically conditioned to its role as unilateral guarantor through the tradition of the Monroe Doctrine, and having previously avoided alliance commitments and consequent disappointments, Americans are less inclined to question the reliability of alliance guarantees than their European partners.

As another example of how different historical experiences may be responsible for shaping different attitudes, one may cite the initially negative European reaction to the American-designed strategy of flexible response. For having only recently emerged from the inferno of a modern conventional war, Europeans displayed a mental block to all rational plans and calculations that considered a similar type of warfare. In this respect one is almost left with the bizarre impression that Europeans prefer nuclear to conventional warfare. It is a case where instinctive preference lies with the worse but unimaginable option of nuclear war rather than with a repetition of experienced and therefore imaginable horrors. In the same manner, Europeans regard the concept of a rationally conducted and consciously directed strategic nuclear war, which underlies the counterforce strategy, not only as a preposterous delusion but also as a threat to the credibility of the deterrent.

Many of NATO's present predicaments, therefore, cannot be explained purely in terms of specific controversial policy issues. Instead, they must be seen as the result of different historical experiences among allies and as the consequence of a considerable expansion of the structural dimensions of traditional alliances in relation to time, space, and number of participants.

The structural components of traditional alliances were characterized by their short-term duration, their narrowly conceived regional orientation, and the relatively small number of participants. In NATO all of these three dimensions have become broadened. This more ambitious expansion has been responsible for the development of some permanent problems in Alliance management. The purpose of Alliance reform might perhaps be served if it were accepted that certain conflicts of interests and incompatibilities, as derived from NATO's basic structural design, are beyond solution and might at best be made more tolerable through adjustment and compromise.

2
Strategic vs Alliance Considerations

IN ADDITION TO the political controversy arising from the structural framework of NATO, there also exists a very fundamental strategic issue, which accounts for a substantial part of present Alliance problems. The issue over Alliance strategy arises from the difficulty of converting NATO from its second strategic phase as an alliance of unilateral deterrence, which no longer satisfies the political aspirations and security needs of its several members, to the status of a community of collective deterrence.

In a strictly bilateral conflict situation the adversary becomes the sole object in the process of developing and applying strategic concepts. Strategic thinking within the forum of a multi-member alliance must acquire an additional dimension. The success of alliance strategy cannot be measured exclusively in terms of its ability to influence and control the behaviour of the adversary. A successful alliance strategy must also be able to reconcile the different security needs of the various members and permit allied participation in the formulation and application of strategic concepts.

COLLECTIVE SECURITY AND COLLECTIVE DEFENCE ASPECTS IN NATO

During its first strategic phase, NATO substantially resembled the traditional concept of a collective defence arrangement. The aggregation of the 12 original members constituted an uncommonly large number of participants, and the creation of a permanent planning machinery in peacetime was without precedent in the annals of alliances. However, the basic aim of NATO allies in seeking to improve their fighting posture by accretion of power and pre-conflict co-ordination conformed with the aims of traditional alliances. In the early phase of NATO, deterrence also followed the classical pattern of establishing a pre-attack advertisement of concerted power, thus indicating to a potential enemy that his objectives would be denied or made too costly.

In some particular aspects, however, the original North Atlantic Treaty may be said to have differed from the model of conventional collective defence arrangements. Collective defence systems are customarily directed against one or a few specifically named or implied adversaries outside the system. The *casus foederis* is either defined in the contractual arrangement, or individual members reserve the right to interpret their obligations under the agreement in accordance with their specific interests in each particular case.

Under collective security arrangements, on the other hand, the nature of the commitment becomes more universal and less subject to independent national interpretation. Collective defence arrangements are designed to meet one specific aggressor. A collective security system is directed against any aggressor, anywhere, at any time within or outside the collective organization. The basis of collective security is not merely a moral-legal condemnation of aggression. The concept is also reinforced by the realization of global interdependence and the threat of escalation of local or regional conflict situations.

Article V of the North Atlantic Treaty (which, incidentally, was modelled on the Rio Pact formula of 1947 and under which members "agree(d) that an armed attack against one or more of them in Europe or North America shall be considered an attack against them all,") reflected the more far-reaching principles of collective security as incorporated in the League Covenant and the UN Charter, rather than the more narrowly defined standards of collective defence under military coalitions. But the collective security aspects of Article V were diluted to collective defence proportions of conventional alliances by the restrictive stipulation under which members reserved the exclusive right to determine the nature of "such actions as [they] deem necessary, including the use of armed force." This caveat indicated that the use of armed force to assist a member against aggression constituted an act of voluntary decision rather than an automatic obligation.

In addition, the treaty formulation of the Atlantic Alliance exceeded traditional alliance commitments insofar as members agreed to "contribute toward the further development of peaceful and friendly international relations by strengthening their free institutions . . . and by promoting conditions of stability and well-being," and to "encourage economic collaboration between any or all of them." As Article II has evolved in practice, however, it constitutes little more than a moral obligation or an expression of aspirations. In fact, the wording of Article II deviates little from the sanctimonious invocations that one customarily finds in the preamble to alliance treaties. As such, its wording may be said to form a liberal 20th century counterpoint to the conservative Holy Alliance.

But despite the affinity of wording, there is the marked distinction that under the North Atlantic Treaty, in contrast to the mere verbal protestations of conventional alliance preambles, there existed the widely held belief that NATO was, indeed, more than a mere military alliance and might be regarded as the first stage in the evolution toward a genuine political and economic community in the North Atlantic area. Combining optimism in the prospects of an evolving Atlantic community with a deeply ingrained suspicion of military alliances, Canadian opinion has consistently voiced this aspiration. Addressing the Canadian House of Commons, prior to the formal signing of the North Atlantic Treaty, the then Secretary of State for External Affairs, Mr. Lester B. Pearson, expressed it as follows:

> In the past, alliances, and leagues, have been formed to meet emergencies and have been dissolved as the emergencies vanished. It must not be so this time. Our Atlantic union must have deeper meaning and deeper roots. It must create conditions for a kind of co-operation which goes beyond the immediate emergency. Threats to peace may bring our Atlantic Pact into existence. Its contribution to welfare and progress may determine how long it is to survive.[1]

Mr. Pearson continued in the same vein when addressing Parliament on February 2, 1951:

> We in Canada hope and believe that the North Atlantic Treaty, founded as it is on the common values of our common civilization, will also grow into something far deeper than any military alliance—into an enduring association among nations which share the same aims and aspirations.[2]

The most notable deviation from traditional alliance behaviour was not so much provided by the North Atlantic Treaty or its immediate aims as by the process of practical implementation with the creation in peacetime of an integrated military planning and command structure in the central sector of Europe. Peacetime integration constituted an entirely novel coalition experiment. SHAPE and its subsidiary regional organizations were set up in response to what was perceived to be an immediate and direct military threat and in realization of the inadequacies of post-attack collective mobilization and planning efforts in the face of the destructiveness and rapidity of modern conventional

---

[1] Canada, House of Commons, *Debates*, February 4, 1949, p. 239.
[2] Canada, House of Commons, *Debates*, p. 52.

warfare. Integration, furthermore, promised to offer the most equitable and harmonious method of pooling and maximizing the defence efforts and of sharing the command functions in an alliance as large as NATO. Smaller allies have regarded integration as the best method of maximizing their individual roles in the over-all process of military planning and decision-making.

PHASE ONE: STRATEGY OF COLLECTIVE DEFENCE

Under the first phase in the strategic evolution of NATO, which may be referred to as a strategy of balanced collective defence, members sought to enhance their individual security posture by pooling their separate forces and by specializing in those aspects of defence for which they were most competent and materially qualified. Under this strategy the defence of Europe was largely envisaged in World War II terms, as a collective allied venture involving conventionally armed forces.

The second strategic phase of the Alliance was dominated by the concept of massive retaliation. In contrast with the collective defence strategy, which represented a communal Alliance venture, the doctrine of massive retaliation was not only the exclusive product of U.S. thinking, but the atomic weapons base which supported it constituted an American monopoly. In its effect on Alliance management, the strategy of deterrence through massive retaliation had the effect of demoting other allies from active participants to passive security consumers.

The impact of the doctrine of massive retaliation has been so strong that the earlier strategic phase is now often forgotten, with the result that several recent commentators have claimed that NATO has never been more than an alliance founded solely on the unilateral guarantee of the United States and its promise to make available its nuclear retaliatory sword in the event of aggression in Europe. The following statement by Ronald Steel mirrors this misconception: "It was, after all, the United States' nuclear guarantee that brought the Europeans into the Alliance in the first place. No one had ever assumed that Europe was to be defended on the ground by conventionally armed troops."[3]

During the first five years of the Alliance, however, it was precisely the organization of a conventional ground defence for Europe which primarily concerned NATO planners. In the light of the subsequent shift of emphasis in favour of the doctrine of massive retaliation, this might seem somewhat incongruous. But it must be realized that during the first few years of NATO the U.S. atomic arsenal and its long-range delivery capability were severely limited, with the result that atomic strikes were regarded in terms of a supporting shield to compensate for the inferiority of conventional forces and not as the conclusive or determining factor of a war in Europe. In the second place, military planners were still under the spell of the environmental influence of World War II operations—the dictum that generals tend to prepare for the next war by fighting the battles of the preceding war has some validity—and therefore constructed a World War III scenario in terms of the experience of the Second World War.

During NATO's initial phase the U.S. guarantee encompassed several related aims. In the first place, the United States sought to deter aggression in Europe by countersigning what was essentially a collective European defence treaty. It has often been claimed that both world wars might have been prevented if it had been known at the outset that the United States would enter on the side of the allies. The American commitment was an application of the traditional form of deterrence by a pre-advertised position which seeks to dissuade a would-be aggressor by demonstrating that his aims would be denied or made too costly. Secondly, the American guarantee was designed as a means of revitalizing Europe's courage and willpower to rebuild its own political institutions and self-defence which had been

[3] Ronald Steel, *The End of Alliance: America and the Future of Europe* (New York: Viking Press, 1964), p. 50.

shattered in the last war. Thirdly, the process of recovery was to be facilitated by direct American economic and military assistance. NATO was designed to complement in the military sphere what the Marshall Plan attempted in the economic sector. Finally, the American monopoly, and later its superiority, in atomic weapons was to act as a shield that would support Western Europe's inferior conventional ground forces until massive military and industrial mobilization could restore conventional parity. While increasing weight was placed on atomic weapons, their use was not regarded as the decisive or terminating factor of a war in Europe.

Instead, the defence of Europe was envisaged in terms of a mixed strategy that involved conventional ground combat in the European area in conjunction with nuclear strikes against the hinterland of the adversary. The increase of U.S. forces in Europe and the dispatching of Canadian troops to the European theatre in 1951 were undertaken with the explicit understanding that this constituted a temporary emergency measure to meet the immediate crisis, but that "fundamentally, and on a long-term basis, each important geographical area must be defended primarily by the people of that region."[4] Expressed in other words, this meant that Europeans were expected to assume the major burden for their own defence.

As no independent nuclear national defence forces were then envisaged for any European member of NATO within the near future, this statement clearly indicates that military thinking anticipated a principally European defence effort by conventional means. The same strategy was enunciated by Marshal Juin, who declared that the atomic bomb was indeed a discouraging reality for the enemy camp but that its use alone could not prevent the enemy from "throwing forward his hordes upon our territory in a reflex action."

---

[4] General Dwight D. Eisenhower's First Report as SACEUR to the Chairman of the NATO Standing Group. Cited in the *New York Times*, April 2, 1952.

According to Juin, only a peacetime coalition of allied forces in Europe could guard the passage of the Rhine.[5]

The aim of preparing for a collective defence of Europe by principally conventional means was reflected by the Lisbon force goals of 1952 which set a target of 96 divisions for the end of 1954, some 35 or 40 of which were to be in a state of immediate combat readiness. The increase of conventional forces as envisaged by the Lisbon goals, however, was not intended as a substitute for the immediate use of nuclear weapons in order "to respond by limited means to a partial attack", as one recent writer indicates.[6] The strategy of flexible response, which underlies this reasoning, had not yet achieved currency in 1952, and all thinking was concentrated on the eventuality of a massive Soviet attack rather than on the contingency of small probing actions or partial aggression. Instead, the force increase was intended for the purpose of implementing the strategy of forward defence. During the first few years of NATO, the limited number of available conventional forces hardly allowed for more ambitious plans than the formation of a covering screen that would fight a withdrawal action, while awaiting mobilization in the shadow of nuclear strikes. But a strategy which envisaged their capture and subsequent liberation had little attraction for the European allies. They could hardly be induced to undertake a major rearmament programme for the sake of such dismal projects. The Lisbon force goals tried to remedy this situation by laying the groundwork for a forward defence posture which would make it possible to hold most of the territory of the European allies during the period following the initial attack. The forward defence strategy at that time did not, however, make alterations in the existing

[5] *Times* (London), April 6, 1953. To some extent, of course, the emphasis on conventional forces and the partial minimization of the effects of atomic weapons reflected the natural desire to encourage Europeans in their conventional military build-up.

[6] Albert Legault, *Deterrence and the Atlantic Alliance* (Toronto: Canadian Institute of International Affairs, 1966), p. 33.

plans for simultaneous nuclear strikes and post-attack mobilization.

PHASE TWO: THE STRATEGY OF UNILATERAL DETERRENCE

Despite serious and moral and strategic reservations, the transition from the early phase of collective defence to that of unilateral deterrence was made with relative speed and did not produce any major divisions in the Alliance. For this one might offer several explanations. In the first place, NATO had never been able to escape from a certain degree of uncertainty whether it served as the instrument for collective defence or merely as the framework for a unilateral nuclear guarantee. While the United States genuinely strove to assist in the formation of a collective defence capability for Europe, its allies, despite formal adherence to this plan, seemed more concerned with capitalizing on the American guarantee. Their contribution to the conventional forces became increasingly regarded as an expensive, albeit necessary, method of preventing the withdrawal of American forces from Europe, the presence of which was regarded as an essential factor in preserving U.S. willingness to underwrite Europe's security with its nuclear guarantee and in making this guarantee seem credible to the enemy.[7] What-

---

[7] Henry Kissinger in *The Troubled Partnership* (New York: McGraw-Hill, 1965), pp. 107-8, offers a most thorough analysis of this strategic ambiguity between the two continental sectors of the Alliance. While his explanation is entirely convincing when it applies to the era which was dominated by the strategy of massive retaliation, one may question whether this split in Alliance thinking was altogether as static throughout the entire period. It would seem that at the outset appreciation for the then restricted atomic capability of the U.S., to say nothing of the tendency to continue along the lines of experienced warfare, promoted genuine consensus in Europe in favour of organizing a collective conventional defence posture. But European support for this strategy diminished more rapidly than it did in the United States, probably less on account of rigorous strategic analysis than because of the economic and political inconveniences that were being encountered in the initial effort of implementing the Lisbon force goals.

ever strategic objections might have been put forward, these offered no adequate counterweight to overriding economic inducements. In fact, allies did not fail to point out that an overly ambitious programme of conventional rearmament would reduce the welfare of their people and might impair public support for free institutions, therby running counter to the very aims of the Alliance as expressed in Article II of the Treaty.

If the New Look strategy offered welcome relief from the economic dilemma of a hard-pressed alliance, it nevertheless entailed an inherent and long-term mortgage on allied cohesion. Even the most effective formula for the sharing of burdens and for participation in planning functions under a strategy of collective defence cannot altogether avoid certain strains within an alliance. These strains arise from the inequitable distribution of power and influence and from the lasting demand on members to make material sacrifices and to adhere to political compromise solutions under a diminishing external threat. Despite these obstacles, the system of collective defence constituted a distinctly useful instrument for alliance management. Collective defence, especially after the implementation of an integrated defence machinery in Europe, resembled a joint stock company in which several members with different stock holdings could participate jointly. Even smaller members could actively involve themselves by contributing conventional forces to one particular sector of NATO or by making military bases and harbour facilities available on their territory. In return for their efforts they were given more than proportional representation on the staff and planning groups of the Alliance. The principal merit of a collective defence system as a feature of alliance policy lay in the fact that it lent itself to some form of equitable distribution of burdens and responsibilities among its numerous members.

The unilateral deterrence phase, however, largely reversed these conditions. The emphasis shifted from a jointly supported and operated conventional force to a nuclear force which was unilaterally owned and controlled by the

United States. The security of the other allies, consequently, rested solely on the credibility of the unilateral American nuclear guarantee. Under such a strategy, security became less a product of active participation in the creation of a collective NATO defence force and in decisions affecting the latter than a matter of passive and skeptical expectation.

Implicit in an alliance strategy based on a monopoly of ownership and control of nuclear weapons is the tendency toward "decollectivization" of joint operational and strategic planning. Apart from the nuclear monopoly, the tendency toward centralization in allied military planning and decision-making functions is furthermore supported by the necessity to counteract the threat of intercontinental or medium-range ballistic missiles, not only by the maintenance of a similar strike and counterstrike force but also by the ability to decide on its use almost instantly. This involves the need for a highly centralized decision-making and control machinery. In the absence of a central executive authority in NATO, decisions affecting the allied strategy of deterrence are largely made by the United States alone and not, necessarily, with reference to the international NATO environment. Even if the military rationale of such strategy were to remain unchallenged, as it clearly was not, the exclusion of allied participation involves inevitable political problems in the management of NATO.

The nature of decisions under a conventional collective defence system differs from that of a nuclear deterrence system. In the former, decisions are not of the same immediacy and consequence as those confronting the authority in control of the nuclear trigger, and thus the very nature of decisions is more gradual, more in the form of a continuous process, and less subject to an automatic retaliatory reflex action. Consequently consulation is still possible under a collective conventional defence system and a degree of sharing or regional allotment of decision-making remains feasible. In a nuclear deterrence system, and form of multinational sharing raises insurmountable obstacles.

The strategy of deterrence, moreover, rests on psychological uncertainties and imponderables which, though exploitable for purely military purposes, make it less than an ideal strategy within an alliance environment. As an instrument of successful alliance policy, a strategy of deterrence must serve the dual purpose of deterring the enemy and of reassuring other allies. Under the strategy of flexible response the capability to deter is strengthened precisely because of the adversary's uncertainty about the conditions under which nuclear weapons would be used. While this element of uncertainty may be strategically effective, it can easily develop into a source of insecurity for allies, especially if the latter are excluded from those decisions which determine the use of nuclear weapons.

Under the collective defence phase, allies gained a feeling of security from the certainty which accompanied the physical presence of integrated forces, and especially of U.S. forces, in the central sector of Europe. Uncertainty, as it existed, related to the military effectiveness of these forces, but it did not involve doubts about their eventual use in a crisis and their deployment according to jointly formulated plans. While the presence of U.S. forces in Europe enhances the credibility of the U.S. guarantee, it offers no absolute assurance that the United States will resort to nuclear weapons in defending Europe and that such weapons will be used strictly in conformity with the priorities of the European allies.

Uncertainty and suspicion characterize relations between adversaries. A strategy directed against an adversary will not only have to take this into account but should also seek to manipulate these uncertainty factors to one's own strategic advantages. But a strategy which is designed to guide the conduct of an entire alliance must guard against the risk of letting these uncertainty factors, which are designed to deter an adversary, discourage and divide the members of an alliance.

The difference between a strategy that was conceived purely in terms of its maximum deterrent effect on the adversary and a strategy which also gave consideration to its wider implications or alliance cohesion was not immediately felt. But this brief period of relative complementarity of interests between European security demands and American strategy was negatively affected by developments on both sides of the Atlantic. On the European side, new demands were being formulated which aimed at terminating Europe's inferior status as a protectorate. The European efforts did not follow the direction of using their regained economic strength and stability as the basis to support an increased integrated conventional defence force, which, in a specialization of functions, would supplement the United States nuclear force. Having themselves become adherents to the doctrine of massive retaliation, the European allies did not seek to alter the strategy but to win for themselves a substantial role in its direction. This was to be achieved either by winning a place of active participation in those nuclear decisions which affected their own security or, this failing, by influencing U.S. decisions indirectly through the expedient of independent national nuclear forces.

On the American side, two principal factors contributed to the breakdown of European acquiescence in the unilateral U.S. custody over the deterrent. The prerequisite for this acquiescence had been American strategic invulnerability and, following from it, the high credibility of the guarantee. This particular condition of the guarantee disappeared with the breakdown of North American continental invulnerability. Expressing himself on this point in his press conference of January 14, 1963, General de Gaulle explained that as long as the United States had an adequate nuclear arsenal and was itself invulnerable to nuclear attack, and showed the will to use nuclear weapons in the defence of Europe, the deterrent had been effective and the question of aggression had scarcely entered French minds. These conditions, however, had lapsed now that the United States was itself vulnerable to nuclear threats. "In these conditions, no one in the world—particularly no one in America—can say if, where, when, how, and to what extent the American nuclear weapons would be employed to defend Europe."[8] Comments by American political figures tended to substantiate rather than alleviate Europe's fears. On April 21, 1959, Christian Herter made the much advertised comment that he could not "conceive of any President involving us in an all-out nuclear war unless the facts showed clearly we are in danger of all-out devastation ourselves."[9] Mr. Herter's comment prompted Dean Acheson's pessimistic prediction that "Europe had its answer."

The other event was the development by U.S. military and political planners of the strategy of flexible response, which entailed at least a partial return to the first phase of collective conventional defence. Or, more correctly, it involved a synthesis of pure unilateral nuclear deterrence and collective defence. Arguments in favour of adopting a more flexible system of military options that could cope with conflict situations beyond the NATO periphery or minor confrontations in Europe became increasingly frequent in the late 1950's. Especially active in this move were officers of the U.S. army, like General Maxwell Taylor, who feared that the preponderant emphasis on nuclear warfare had left their particular service critically weak for this type of commitment where the army would be called upon to play a major role.

[8] French Embassy, Press and Information Division, *Major Addresses, Statements and Press Conferences of General Charles de Gaulle, 1958-1964,* p. 217.

[9] U.S. Senate, Committee on Foreign Relations, 86th Congress, 1st Session, *Hearings on the Nomination of Christian A. Herter to be Secretary of State,* pp. 9-10. Taking counsel of their worst fears, Europeans probably misinterpreted Secretary Herter's statement. The latter had realistically predicted that the United States would not engage in nuclear war in response to a minor probing action in Europe or an isolated incident. This did not mean, however, that the United States would refuse to enter into nuclear war, if, in consideration of its interdependence with Europe, such an attack was judged to be a prelude to a nuclear attack against American territory or the beginning of an inevitable chain reaction that would culminate in an attack of this nature. In such a case the U.S. might have been prompted to resort to a pre-emptive nuclear strike.

In the eyes of the Eisenhower Administration these dissenting views were criticized as being parochial and sectarian. But in the October 1957 issue of *Foreign Affairs*, which coincided with the launching of *Sputnik*, Mr. Dulles, the archangel of the nuclear sword, introduced a variation on his nuclear theme, when he predicted that

> in contrast to the 1950 decade, it may be that by the 1960 decade the nations which are around the Sino-Soviet perimeter can possess an effective defence against full-scale conventional attack and thus confront any aggressor with the choice between failing or himself initiating nuclear war against the defending country.[10]

Significantly, however, the possibility of a conventional defence posture which Mr. Dulles held out relied entirely on the use of tactical nuclear weapons which were then practically equated with conventional weapons.

The transition from the strategy of massive retaliation, where the conventional shield forces in Europe had almost become reduced to a tripwire role to verify the occurrence of an attack and to give the signal for an automatic Pavlovian nuclear response, to the McNamara strategy of flexible response was made by the Norstad Plan, which might be termed a strategy of graduated retaliation. The nature of the Norstad Plan was unveiled in two major speeches in 1957.[11] While denying the possibility of defending Europe conventionally against a massive attack, General Norstad called for the increase of ground forces in Western Europe to thirty divisions and their equipment with tactical nuclear weapons. This force was designed to cope with local probing actions and incidents without resorting to massive retaliation, or, to use Norstad's phrase, "to meet less-than-ultimate threats with a decisive, but less-than-ultimate response." Underlying the Norstad Plan was the concept of

[10] John Foster Dulles, "Challenge and Response in U.S. Policy", *Foreign Affairs*, Vol. 36, No. 1 (October 1957), p. 31.

[11] General Lauris Norstad's address to the American Council on NATO, New York, January 29, 1957, cited in *NATO Letter*, V, No. 2 (February 1957), pp. 27-30. Address at Cincinnati, November 12, 1957, cited in *NATO Letter*, V, No. 12 (December 1957), pp. 26-28.

the "pause" and its strategic twin, the "threshold". By increasing the conventional shield forces, enemy assaults could be withstood at least temporarily, thus showing allied determination to resist and enforcing a pre-nuclear pause that would allow the enemy time to reconsider its decision in the light of this determination. The "pause" was to be regarded more as a concept than a definite period of time. In the same manner, attempts at seeking victory by "salami" tactics, that is by a series of limited *faits accomplis*, at low escalation risks, could be thwarted by an increased shield force. If the adversary were still bent on crossing this heightened threshold in the pursuit of his restricted aims he would be forced to invest considerably higher force levels, thus foregoing the advantages of a surprise move and substantially adding to the risk of escalation.

The concepts of the Norstad Plan were brought to their ultimate conclusion by the introduction of the strategy of flexible response of which Defence Secretary McNamara has emerged as chief exponent. The principal characteristic of the McNamara doctrine has been the multiplication of available options and the clear differentiation between various responses. The Norstad Plan had thought of a nuclear response in terms of all-out retaliation and of conventional defence largely in conjunction with tactical nuclear weapons. The McNamara approach envisaged the application of strategic nuclear forces in a variety of ways that ranged from mere threats to their actual use against enemy military installations (counterforce strategy) or, finally, against centres of civilization (countercity strategy). In the same manner, the conventional defence posture in Europe was to be improved to a level that would enable NATO to meet limited provocations by a purely conventional effort, without resorting to tactical nuclear weapons simply because NATO had "no other way to cope with a particular situation."[12]

---

[12] Defence Secretary Robert McNamara, testimony before the House Armed Services Committee, *The Fiscal Years 1964-68, Defense Program and 1964 Defense Budget*, January 30, 1963, p. 18.

The separation of conventional from tactical nuclear weapons did not imply that the latter were to be taken out of circulation—in fact, U.S. stocks of tactical nuclear weapons in Europe experienced an uninterrupted build-up—but that the decision relating to their use would be made strictly on over-all strategic considerations and not in default of other options.

Apart from the physical multiplication of options, the principal feature of the new strategy lay in its psychological manipulation of the uncertainty of response as a means of controlling or restricting the moves of the adversary. This was in strong contradiction to the pre-advertised certainty under the declaratory policy in the era of massive retaliation. The new concept was based on the argument that an overly precise declaration of the nature of the particular response to each act of aggression might create a set of graduated and predictable ceilings, in the recognizable confines of which enemy planners could manoeuvre with relative protection from the risk of escalation. Defence Secretary McNamara explained it in the following terms:

> Our new policy gives us the flexibility to choose among several operational plans, but does not require that we make any advance commitment with respect to doctrine or targets. We shall be committed only to a system that gives us the ability to use our forces in a controlled and deliberate way, so as best to pursue the interests of the United States, our Allies, and the rest of the Free World.[13]

While this approach provided distinct advantages in dealing with adversaries, it imposed serious strains on U.S. relations with her NATO allies. Apart from the instinctive fear that a renewed emphasis on collective defence might constitute a masked nuclear disengagement by the United States, or might at least convey this impression, and thus reduce the credibility of the deterrent, the strategy of unde-

[13] Robert S. McNamara, address before the Fellows of the American Bar Foundation Dinner, Chicago, February 17, 1962. Cited in Henry Kissinger, *op. cit.*, p. 99.

clared response and purposely sustained uncertainty intensified allied insecurity complexes. Deeply suspicious from experience and conscious of their vulnerability to any type of warfare in Europe, the European members of the North Atlantic Alliance had sought to satisfy their natural craving for security by enlisting the unquestioned and irrevocable U.S. commitment to respond to any form of aggression in Europe by an automatic massive nuclear strike, regardless of the rationality of the response. The McNamara strategy, however, was precisely designed to restore the rationality of decision-making, to multiply the range of available options, and to increase the time factor for crisis bargaining.

PROBLEMS OF FUNCTIONAL SPECIALIZATION UNDER A STRATEGY OF FLEXIBLE RESPONSE

During NATO's collective defence phase, when the U.S. nuclear force was regarded as a support function for the major sword action of the collective conventional forces in Europe, a system of continental specialization of functions might have represented a valid proposition for Alliance management. Under this strategy the central effort would have been conventional. Direction and decision-making would therefore have largely remained in the hands of the European powers, which would have contributed the major portion to the conventional sword.

The strategy of flexible response, however, is a deterrence strategy. Instead of assigning to nuclear weapons a role in support of conventional forces, as was originally envisaged, conventional forces now serve the function of upholding the credibility of the deterrent at low levels of conflict. Under this strategy every aspect of warfare, down to the most restricted conventional engagement, involves the threat of the use or consideration of the use or non-use of the nuclear deterrent. In consequence, every type of modern warfare, and especially every military conflict in the vital European sector, constitutes a nuclear war regardless of whether nuclear weapons are actually employed or whether their use remains reserved. Because of the industrial and urban concentration in Europe and the relative limitation of available forces, the defence of Western Europe can no longer be conceived of in terms of conventional weapons. But under given circumstances a conflict could be waged temporarily by conventional means and the adversary's objective be denied, if there existed an uninterrupted circuit that linked this conventional force to the nuclear deterrent. In this way, the above conflict would to a certain measure become a nuclear war waged with conventional weapons.

However, in order to provide for such an uninterrupted circuit, those allies manning the conventional forces should also be given some form of participation in the strategic planning and decision-making process relating to the use of nuclear weapons. A functional division of labour, as envisaged by U.S. strategists under the concept of flexible response, where Europeans would provide the integrated conventional forces while the United States retained exclusive control over the use of the nuclear deterrent, can no longer be regarded as an acceptable alternative for the North Atlantic Alliance. On both shores of the Atlantic unpleasant truths must be faced. The United States must accept that its European allies will not be induced to improve their conventional force commitments without being allowed a voice in the management of the nuclear deterrent which will determine the efficacy of the former, while Europeans cannot reasonably expect U.S. forces to be stationed on European soil in perpetuity if they themselves deny the strategic rationale that determines their continued presence in Europe.

Strategic and economic considerations might well argue in favour of retaining the present specialization of alliance functions with respect to production, financing, and manning, where the U.S. keeps a nuclear force and the European allies provide the integrated conventional machinery. But this specialization cannot also be carried over into the stage that concerns itself with over-all nuclear planning, strategy formulation, and certain aspects of nuclear decision-making. If the doctrine of flexible response is to be politically tolerable to a multinational alliance, a functional as distinct from a mere formal representational role must be reserved for the other NATO allies in determining the latter stage. This inevitably raises the question of nuclear control in the Alliance.

3

NATO and the Nuclear Control Problem

A PRELIMINARY NOTE of caution ought to be inserted before embarking on a chapter concerned with the issue of nuclear control in NATO. In dealing with this subject it is necessary to avoid the impression that all Alliance questions may be directly attributed to the nuclear control issue, and that all problems would find their ultimate solution with an adequate settlement of the nuclear problem. As was indicated in the preceding chapters, there exist numerous fundamental structural and psychological issues in the North Atlantic Alliance which not only chronologically precede but also transcend the nuclear control question. The reduction of all NATO problems to a common nuclear control denominator might promote undue optimism about solving all Alliance questions in conjunction with the nuclear riddle, or lead to an unduly pessimistic evaluation of NATO's future prospects if the nuclear control problem does not find an adequate solution in the near future. It would, furthermore, detract from the study of other key issues of policy in NATO.

Despite this caveat, the central position which the nuclear problem occupies in NATO policy cannot be ignored. Just as all roads may be said to lead to Rome, so at least the majority of the principal questions now confronting the Alliance converge on the issue of nuclear control.

The centralization of ownership and control over nuclear weapons conflicts with the established NATO practice of sharing the burdens and responsibilities of defence collectively. One might rationally argue that other members of NATO could provide a nuclear contribution in the form of direct financial subsidies to the construction of the U.S. nuclear force. However, this proposition can hardly be regarded as a viable Alliance project, for, reminiscent of the declining Delian League, it would transform the Alliance from an organization that is voluntarily supported by the active participation of its several members to an association of subservient states rendering an annual tribute to their Athenian master.

FOUR NUCLEAR THEMES IN NATO

One may abstract at least four basic patterns of thought from the multiple variations which exist on the NATO nuclear theme. The first of these supports the concept of a nuclear monopoly within the Alliance in pursuance of a strategy of functional specialization. This would accord to the United States a nuclear role and the obligation to underwrite the security of its other NATO allies by a nuclear guarantee, while assigning to the latter the responsibility for supporting a collective conventional defence force in Europe.

The second theme is that of nuclear multipolarity within NATO. The *de facto* base for multipolarity has already been provided by the emergence of independent national nuclear forces in Britain and France. This development has superseded the phase of nuclear monopoly, even though U.S. policy and strategic thinking has shown considerable reluctance to give "diplomatic" recognition to this *de facto* situation, especially as it involves the *force de frappe*, and frequently treats the present situation as an extension of the previous era of monopoly.

The concept of a European nuclear force represents the third theme of nuclear thinking in the Alliance. Exponents of this particular plan have taken cognizance of the existence of nuclear multipolarity in NATO but have shown concern lest these separate national nuclear forces in Europe be militarily ineffective, proliferation-prone, and politically divisive. Their plan consequently envisages the creation of an independent integrated European nuclear force, which would include the present British and French nuclear components, and which would operate in closest co-operation with the U.S. nuclear force. While envisaging a close partnership between these two forces in the area of planning, technical assistance, and the exchange of information, the European solution insists on retaining two separate centres for nuclear decision-making. These would coexist harmoniously, but they would not merge.

The fourth approach is provided by "Atlanticists" who fear that a separate European nuclear force would be too weak, in view of some inevitable duplication also too costly, and most of all, too loosely tied to the centre of U.S. nuclear decision-making and thus susceptible of being cast adrift from its major partner at the first crisis. They therefore promote the establishment of an integrated Atlantic nuclear force. The latter would be separated from the principal U.S. nuclear striking force, but would combine elements from both sides of the Atlantic into one nuclear venture. It is hoped that this would have a cohesive, rather than a divisive effect on NATO and, furthermore, that it would provide the means of absorbing the independent British and French nuclear efforts and thus eliminate all unilateral centres of nuclear decision-making within the Alliance except the American one.

Two separate streams seem to be emerging within the Atlantic school of thought. The first favours a "hardware" solution, i.e., the physical creation of a NATO nuclear force in which members could jointly participate in all or some of the elements of ownership, manning, direction, and control. The previous MLF and ANF proposals fall into this category. The other solution places less emphasis on the creation of a separate Atlantic nuclear force but concentrates on finding a solution whereby existing or proposed Alliance channels could be used in order to win for the other Alliance members a place for active participation in those aspects of planning, strategic formulation, and decision-making which have previously been the exclusive preserve of the United States. The latter approach underlies the seven-member NATO nuclear planning group which was established in December of 1966, following a proposal which Defence Secretary McNamara had made at the 1965 meeting of NATO Defence Ministers.

The allied desire for a greater role in nuclear policy stems from considerations of security as well as from concern about prestige and economic and technological progress. According to the French Minister of Defence, Pierre Messmer, the *force de frappe* represents not only "an irreplacable factor of scientific, technological, and industrial progress", but also the prerequisite to the expression of a "legitimate national point of view".[1] However, in resolving the already excruciatingly complex problem of nuclear control in a multinational setting, the principal concern must be with the question of allied security rather than with psychological needs for prestige and independence or with economic considerations, all the more as the latter may be resolved, in part at least, by other methods.

THE NATURE OF THE THREAT TO NATO

Insofar as the nuclear issue in NATO arises largely from allied concern with security, it leads us to question the nature of the military threat which confronts members of the Alliance. In this era of partial *détente* with the Soviet Union, the very belief in the existence of a threat is some-

---

[1] Pierre Messmer, "The French Military Establishment of Tomorrow", *Orbis*, VI, No. 2 (Summer 1962), p. 206.

times portrayed as a manipulated phenomenon that is artificially preserved by the founders of NATO who are said to have a vested interest in the perpetuation of the organization of their creation, with the result that the cold-war climate is unnecessarily and artificially sustained. In the case of a defensive alliance, as is the case with preventive medicine, it is difficult to establish the degree of effectiveness of the measure taken, for success might be attributed to inherent immunity as much as to the remedy.

The formation of NATO represented a joint response to the effects of an unprecedented westward expansion under Stalin of Soviet territorial possessions and influence, all within less than a decade. In his policy Stalin combined callous opportunism with a cautious temperament. The extension of the Communist domain under his leadership in the majority of cases was achieved through the ruthless exploitation of existing opportunities rather than by overt aggression. Until the unlikely day when the Kremlin archives will be opened and the old guard of Soviet leaders publish their memoirs, it will always remain an open question whether Stalin had, in fact, contemplated aggression in Western Europe and was restrained by the formation of NATO. Even if that question remains unanswered, there can be little doubt that without the creation of NATO, the Soviet Union would have exploited the situation of Europe's division and dislocation in order to expose the West European powers to a barrage of threats, pressures, and intimidating measures, accompanied by internal interference through the pliable instrument of the local Communist parties. Short of culminating in a Communist takeover, such parallel efforts would have impaired Europe's programme of economic and political recovery as well as the process of reconciliation between former enemies.

If the Kremlin leadership of today seems less willing to exercise the option of applying force to extend its system of government and its sphere of influence beyond the present periphery—ends which are not merely attributed to Moscow but are openly proclaimed and defended by the latter—it is in realization of the reduced opportunities and the vastly increased risks under the existing super-power nuclear equilibrium. As noted by Alastair Buchan,

> No responsible person in the West would be prepared to argue that the increasing implausibility of a Soviet military attack on Western Europe is the result of any fundamental change of heart in Moscow, let alone the perfection of that flexible system of military options in Western Europe which military analysts have long regarded as desirable. The greater confidence in the stability of the East-West confrontation in Europe arises very largely from the stabilization of military technology.[2]

The practice of peaceful coexistence does not eliminate conflict but reduces it to less hazardous forms in order to avoid the risk of massive confrontation. Nor does peaceful coexistence rule out conflict by military means, inasmuch as the Soviet Union has pledged to lend its support to wars of "national liberation", a euphemistic description for indirect aggression. Even without any super-power instigation there may be an emergence of regional conflict situations that would correspond neither to the time nor place of their choosing, yet involve the super-powers on a collision course, as both sides pursue their more far-reaching commitments.

As the result of the nuclear equilibrium, these conflicts in the third world are conducted in a relatively controlled environment, but no amount of carefully supervised strategic experiments can offer genuine assurance against a degree of escalation that would involve the European members of NATO. But basically the threat to the security of NATO's European allies has its nucleus in the situation in Europe itself and not in Asia or Africa.

The creation of a genuine system of security in Europe would depend on the realization of all, or at least some, of the following features: the emergence of a "security community" between Eastern and Western Europe; the establishment of a reasonable distribution or balance of power be-

[2] Alastair Buchan, "The Changed Setting of the Atlantic Debate," *Foreign Affairs*, Vol. 44, No. 2 (July 1965), p. 577.

tween Western Europe and Eastern Europe and the Soviet Union; and a political settlement in Europe that would be acceptable to both sides.

A "security community", to use Karl Deutsch's concept, denotes a group of nations that have become sufficiently integrated through institutions and the exercise of informal practices to permit the expectation of peaceful change for the foreseeable future.[3] The security of such a community depends not on factors of deterrence but on commonly shared values which allow for the peaceful settlement or adjudication of conflicting interests. It is precisely this community of interests and values which characterizes U.S.-Canadian relations and which explains the Canadian feeling of security *vis-à-vis* the United States. It would be entirely unrealistic to ascribe Canadian security to its ability to deter by military means a possible American aggression. However, even the most optimistic calculations would hesitate to characterize the present tenuous and partial *détente* between Eastern Europe and Western Europe as the existence of a "security community".

In the absence of such community and without compatible interests more far-reaching than the desire to avoid mutual annihilation, nations instinctively seek to pool their strength in order to create a counterbalance of force that might be able to deter aggression or pressure from the side of their preponderant neighbour. The present power position of the Soviet Union in conjunction with its East European client states is such that no West European power combination could sufficiently outweigh it without support from the United States. As one German commentator has recently noted,

> It is a Gaullist delusion that it is possible for Western Europe, as it was during the nineteenth century, to maintain a stable equilibrium with Eastern Europe on a quite independent basis. The old balance cannot be reestablished—simply because the old scales have been toppled

---

[3] Karl Deutsch *et al.*, *Political Community and the North Atlantic Area* (Princeton, N.J.: Princeton University Press, 1957), p. 5.

over. In the thermo-nuclear age, Western Europe can make up for the disadvantages of its geography only by a close and indissoluble alliance with the United States.[4]

Even in the unlikely case that the Gaullist view, which envisages a gradual disintegration of Communism and the return of the Soviet Union to the status of a "normal" nation state, were true, Western Europe would find it necessary to seek an equitable balance against the adjacent super-power. Before having established a "security community" with this super-power, whether of Communist or nationalist orientation, Western Europe would almost intuitively seek to protect itself against this aggregation of power by maintaining an adequate counterbalance. Without this protection the Soviet Union could exert military pressure on the West European powers and subject them to a long list of demands, such as their withdrawal from NATO, the dissolution of the European Economic Community, and a closer association with a Soviet-dominated economic community.

Finally, European insecurity stems from the absence of a legitimate postwar settlement in Europe. The Congress of Vienna may serve as a model of a legitimate political settlement which accomplished a judicious accommodation of conflicting interests and thus created the basis for a lasting peace. The present European condition, in contrast, may be characterized as a crystallization of the *status quo*. But while the apparently immobile situation at the height of the cold war seemed to lend to this non-settlement the appearance of stability, the centrifugal effects of the present nuclear equilibrium have once again exposed the explosive nature of this arbitrarily improvised situation. In this most strategic sector of the world, such vital questions as the status of Berlin, Germany's reunification, and her relations with her eastern neighbours, as well as the boundaries and relations of the East European powers among themselves and with the Soviet Union, have been left unsettled. While

---

[4] Theo Sommer, "For an Atlantic Future", *Foreign Affairs*, Vol. 43, No. 1 (Oct. 1964), p. 114.

countries such as Poland, Czechoslovakia, and Rumania will hardly be in a position to exercise their revisionist demands against the Soviet Union, centrifugal tendencies within Eastern Europe may lead to a situation where such demands will be exercised against each other, with resulting instability to all of Europe. In the same manner, the potential conflict between the Federal Republic of Germany and East Germany, especially over the delicate Berlin issue, might be increased if East Germany became less dependent on Soviet assistance and thus less subject to Moscow's restraining influence.

Under these circumstances the perception of a threat is not unfounded. Europe's security can be cemented by a laborious process through the common Alliance framework. It cannot be taken for granted. Dean Acheson, with customary bluntness, admonishes those Europeans who take their security for an automatic gift of Providence: "In 1949 they did not have security; now they do have it, and, having it, they think it is an act of God; it just happens to good Europeans. It doesn't. It happens because of the success of NATO."[5]

The desire of the European allies for an expanded nuclear role naturally applies most strongly to those contingencies in which the U.S. deterrent has a low level of credibility. Low deterrence credibility applies neither to a massive nuclear attack against the North American continent nor, as long as a basic community of interests exists between America and Europe, to a similar attack against Western Europe. A distinctly lower level of deterrence credibility, however, would apply to situations involving either a large-scale conventional attack against Western Europe that could not be withstood by NATO's existing conventional forces, or selective nuclear strikes against one particular ally. The last contingency would be particularly relevant to

---

[5] Dean Acheson, *The Crisis in NATO*, hearings before the Subcommittee on Europe of the Committee on Foreign Affairs, House of Representatives (89th Congress, 2nd Session), May 17, 1966, p. 191.

situations where the initial crisis had been provoked by a member of NATO through actions that were not sanctioned by the rest of the Alliance.[6] In such circumstances the United States would be faced with the particularly difficult choice of risking nuclear retaliation against itself through its assistance to a deviant ally.

The European demand for a greater share in nuclear decision-making in such situations is not only supported by doubts about the credibility of the existing deterrent but also by the realization that it is precisely situations of this nature that may offer sufficient time to make feasible allied consultation and collective decision-making on questions of nuclear defence. The search for a solution of the nuclear control problem in NATO should, therefore, be concentrated on the two most relevant aspects of the common nuclear defence: the determination of the circumstances under which nuclear weapons are to be used if a conventional defence should prove inadequate, and the application of the threat or the actual use of nuclear weapons in the event of an isolated nuclear provocation against a particular ally.

[6] One may envisage the following situation: The German border police has become engaged in hostilities with East German border guards in order to assist East German refugees. German opinion becomes sufficiently aroused that units of the German army are advanced to assist its border police, despite opposition by other NATO members to this course of action. At this stage the Soviet Union actively intervenes by presenting Germany with an ultimatum demanding that the German regular forces withdraw to a more westward position than previously occupied by them as a guarantee against repetition of the incident. The ultimatum further threatens to engage in selective tactical nuclear strikes against certain targets on West German territory, if the Federal Republic refuses to comply. The precipitate and unilateral German action has isolated her from the rest of the Alliance. The Soviet Union exploits this temporary split by assuring all other members that it has no hostile intentions against them. The Alliance would be faced with a real dilemma.

It must be admitted, however, that situations of this kind have occupied American strategic thinkers rather than Europeans, who would assign little credibility to their possible occurrence.

INDEPENDENT NUCLEAR FORCES

The development of the British and French nuclear forces has irrevocably altered the original condition of a nuclear monopoly within the Atlantic Alliance. Even though political and technological motives have largely shaped the decision in favour of developing these so-called independent nuclear forces, most of the arguments that have been made to justify their existence have been couched in strategic terms.

General Gallois, the apologist of the *force de frappe,* has sketched a scene of Hobbesian anarchy where all the alliances and relevant collective deterrent arrangements have lost their credibility. According to General Gallois, nuclear conditions have created a form of universal equality of opportunity insofar as former differentials of strategic location, space, and economic resources have become virtually eliminated by the arrival of universal nuclear vulnerability, when even smaller nuclear powers can deter super-powers by virtue of their ability to inflict unacceptable damage on the latter. According to this argument, all powers enjoying the necessary economic and technological capacity would create their own nuclear force and thus join the assembly of nuclear peers.

In the opinion of Raymond Aron, the Gallois doctrine of deterrence "is a fatal rehash of the massive retaliation concept, and it is a miniature version ten years behind the times."[7] While the threat of massive retaliation is the only strategic course available to a small and vulnerable first-strike nuclear force of the French variety, it seems totally unrealistic to urge super-powers with a second-strike capability and a range of available options "to go back to Dulles' forthright pledge" of all-or-nothing massive retaliation.[8] Even in the unlikely case that the United States should formally resume its pledge of massive retaliation under any

[7] Raymond Aron, *The Great Debate* (Garden City, N.J.: Doubleday, 1965), p. 98.

[8] Pierre Gallois, "U.S. Strategy and the Defense of Europe", *Orbis*, VII, No. 2 (Summer 1963), p. 248.

circumstances, such verbal guarantee could not regain a convincing degree of credibility in the calculations of the adversary. To many Alliance members, therefore, the Gallois doctrine must appear as antiquated as Metternich's policy seemed to Talleyrand when he commented that Austria was "toujours en retard d'une politique et d'une guerre."

General de Gaulle shares with General Gallois both the conviction that powers such as France require the means for an independent nuclear decision, and the belief that even a small nuclear force of the style of the *force de frappe* has the capability to deter a super-power by virtue of being able to threaten the latter with damage which would be disproportionate to the adversary's possible gain. A French nuclear force on a counter-city assignment, as President de Gaulle pointed out in his press conference of January 14, 1963, could destroy millions of people in a few seconds, a fact which could not "fail to have at least some bearing on the intents of any possible aggressor."[9]

General de Gaulle's political blueprint seems to envisage a Europe in which French claims to primacy and leadership would be reinforced by her nuclear possession. This embryonic possession is already now being portrayed as conferring distinct security benefits on her European allies. It is interesting to observe that in recent conversations with Soviet leaders, President de Gaulle referred to the fact that France and the U.S.S.R. were the only continental European powers in possession of nuclear weapons. The implication was that this tended to equalize their status and created common interests. But unlike General Gallois, who anticipates the dissolution of alliances and views the actual use of nuclear weapons in an isolated setting between two adversaries, General de Gaulle seeks to exercise an independent national choice in close association and co-operation with the other nuclear powers of NATO, though preferably out-

[9] French Embassy, Press and Information Division, *Major Addresses, Statements and Press Conferences of General Charles de Gaulle, 1958-1964*, p. 218.

side the formal and integrated machinery of the North Atlantic Alliance. The existence of an independent French nuclear capacity, as de Gaulle explained at the above-cited
press conference, did not preclude the combined action of
this force with the nuclear forces of France's allies. But
integration of this nuclear force was "unimaginable" insofar
as it would destroy the capacity for independent nuclear
decision-making.[10]

What has been expressed by President de Gaulle, largely
in terms of political and nationalistic rhetoric, has acquired
a measure of strategic sophistication in the thinking of General André Beaufre and the members of the French Institute
of Strategic Studies who believe they "have brought to light
certain laws concerning multilateral deterrence."[11]

Although both Generals Gallois and Beaufre make the
strategic justification of the French *force de frappe* the centre of their argument, their approaches differ completely.
Gallois proceeds from a position which discounts the validity of alliances in the nuclear age and contemplates the use
of nuclear weapons in sovereign isolation, while Beaufre
justifies an independent French nuclear force precisely because it would operate within the framework of the Atlantic
Alliance. According to General Beaufre, the present danger
arises from the fact that nuclear deterrence has reached
such a stable equilibrium that the risk of the use of nuclear
weapons has been eliminated from virtually every conflict
situation other than all-out nuclear aggression by one super-
power against the other. The result has been a credibility
gap in the deterrent. This gap could be repaired if the adversary were confronted with an element of risk, uncertainty, or even irrationality, which would be provided by

---

[10] *Ibid.*, p. 217.

[11] André Beaufre, "Nuclear Deterrence and World Strategy", cited
in Karl Cerny and Henry Briefs, *op. cit.*, p. 221. For a further elabora-
tion, see General Beaufre's *Dissuasion et Stratégie* (Paris: Armand
Colin, 1964) and his "The Sharing of Nuclear Responsibilities", *International Affairs*, XLI, No. 3 (July 1965), pp. 411-418.

creating independent, though closely co-ordinated, centres for nuclear decision-making within the Alliance. In a crisis situation, these independent nuclear centres pose the risk not only of initiating a first-strike blow but also of "triggering" the American nuclear force. In other words, the existence of an independent nuclear force serves to "confer upon the principal ally's nuclear forces (more or less neutralized by the existing balance)a more extensive deterrent power."[12] The credibility of this strategy of multiple nuclear decision-making centres, according to Beaufre, rests on continued NATO co-operation and co-ordination but not on integration, which would remove the means for independent decisions.

There is a very appealing and convincing logic in General Beaufre's arguments. The addition to existing uncertainties and risks might, under some conditions, represent a positive gain for NATO. Unfortunately nuclear strategy is an exotic plant which vegetates in the greenhouse of paradoxes. On the one hand, nuclear strategy must seek to fortify the deterrent, but on the other hand, it must not succeed too well lest the risk of the potential use of nuclear weapons decline to a level where the deterrent will fail to deter. Similarly, it is important to take all necessary precautions to prevent an escalation of smaller conflicts, but the removal of the fear of escalation might induce powers to take greater risks and to instigate or encourage limited conflict situations from which they might otherwise be dissuaded under more unstable conditions. "Escalation", notes Raymond Aron, "is at once a danger that needs to be met and a threat that could not and should not be surrendered."[13]

In the midst of these paradoxes it becomes an agonizing choice to select the proper strategy. The ultimate aims for security are the same. But one may select one's criteria, and then proceed to circumnavigate the globe of deterrence

[12] André Beaufre, in Karl Cerny and Henry Briefs, *op. cit.*, p. 221.
[13] Raymond Aron, *op. cit.*, p. 216.

from east to west, or one may emphasize other assumptions and set out for the same goal by proceeding on an opposite course. Apart from leaving unanswered such questions as the possible influence on proliferation which the French example may exert on other NATO allies, and its undoubtedly detrimental impact on NATO cohesion, General Beaufre's strategy of multi-polar deterrence is based on the assumption that a nuclear France would not be inhibited by the United States, but that the latter would in all circumstances be constrained to support whatever independent choice France might initiate. The strategy also rests on the assumption that there exists a near-perfect stability in the super-power nuclear balance. The balance of deterrence, however, as presented in Albert Wohlstetter's brilliant analysis,[14] is an extremely delicate instrument with inherent risks, uncertainties, and imbalances. Consequently, any conscious effort to add to these uncertainties would have to be regarded as a perilous venture.

A strategy of multipolar deterrence creates additional risks that could, indeed, dissuade an adversary from purposely initiating a crisis. But underlying the argument is the assumption that the threat to resort to a nuclear first strike against a super-power by a country as vulnerable as France, which would in fact be the promissory note of suicide, could be made to appear convincing.[15] It might, indeed, be

[14] Albert Wohlstetter, "The Delicate Balance of Terror", *Foreign Affairs*, vol. 37, No. 2 (January 1959), pp. 211-235.

[15] "I can never make out", writes Air Marshal Sir John Slessor, (cited in Karl Cerny and Henry Briefs, *op. cit.*, p. 39) "why it should be assumed that Britain would not be deterred from using her nuclear force by the inevitability of complete obliteration of the United Kingdom, but that Russia would be deterred by a far less cataclysmic degree of damage. The credibility of an independent national deterrent requires the capability of inflicting comparative, not relative, damage on the enemy." A difference does, however, exist, insofar as Britain or France would be acting in a mood of total despair and fatalism under extreme provocation, whereas the Soviet Union, being the initiator of the Crisis, and acting from a position of rational calculation, would be less willing to expose itself to injury as the result of its own move.

argued that even in the face of low allied cohesion and the further diminution of the credibility of the U.S. nuclear guarantee, it would still be more natural for the enemy to believe that the United States would initiate nuclear war in the defence of its ally than to expect the latter to choose suicide deliberately. One must also realize that not all conflict situations which involve the threat of nuclear war are deliberately and calculatingly instigated by a super-power. Some crises occur spontaneously, others are provoked by third powers and may unwittingly entangle the super-powers. Panic decisions are more apt to result from situations of this kind than from a controlled challenge by either superpower which follows from a carefully prepared plan. Multiple centres of nuclear decision, added uncertainties, and purposely heightened risks could hardly be regarded as desirable prescriptions for relieving crisis situations of this kind.

Perhaps national nuclear forces of the *force de frappe* genre, like old soldiers, never die but merely fade away. However, the fading process is bound to be a long one and even an adequate solution to NATO's nuclear control problem does not guarantee the demise of these forces. A "hardware" solution in the form of a separate European or Atlantic nuclear force would not necessarily replace these national nuclear efforts by absorbing them into the larger unit. National nuclear forces might conceivably continue to coexist next to the collective unit, or they might be merged with the latter on terms that permitted their independent national use under defined conditions. While President de Gaulle favours a European nuclear force, he has shown no willingness to sacrifice to an integrated European force whatever capacity there may now exist for the independent national use of the *force de frappe*.

The British nuclear force, whose increasing technological dependence on the United States was sealed by the Nassau agreement, has withstood an election campaign which was won on the platform of denuclearization, among other issues.[16] In the Nassau agreement of 1962, it will be recalled, the United States agreed to compensate Britain for the cancellation of the Skybolt programme by providing the planned British nuclear submarine force with American Polaris missiles. In return, Britain pledged to "assign" her V-bomber force and eventually also the planned Polaris-armed submarine force to the North Atlantic Alliance. Britain, however, retained an escape clause which permitted the withdrawal of these forces for independent national use in the event of extreme national emergency. Insofar as there exists no NATO nuclear force as a separate entity, the British nuclear force has retained its national identity despite its "assigned" status. Under its present status, the British V-bomber force is "assigned" to NATO, that is to say, it has become part of SACEUR's planning responsibilities and thus has become a matter of general Alliance concern, but it continues to be nationally owned by the United Kingdom, to be manned by British crews, and to be commanded by British officers. The French *force de frappe* has not been "assigned" to NATO, nor has the present French government shown any indication of its willingness to merge its national nuclear force with a larger NATO force if such a force were to be created.

Whatever strategic arguments may be made in favour of multiple, *force de frappe* style, nuclear forces within the Atlantic Alliance, there seems to be no convincing strategic rationale for their application beyond the NATO periphery in "an east of Suez" type of policy as outlined by the British Defence White Paper of 1965. In the first place, these forces are too small to permit any scattering for commitments on a global scale. Also the risk of actually using these weapons would be so great, and in no way commensurate with their owners' political involvement in these regions, that the de-

[16] In a television address in March 1964, Harold Wilson, then leader of the Opposition, outlined the future of British defence policy if the Labour Party were to form the next government: "Yes, there is no ambiguity, Britain will cease this pretence of being a nuclear power." Cited in the *Globe and Mail*, March 10, 1964.

terrent effect of such commitments could hardly be more than fractional.

It is therefore unlikely that a country like India would, for any extended period, be willing to regard a guarantee involving a few British V-bombers as an adequate counterbalance to Chinese nuclear threats. Only her association with either or both super-powers could provide the necessary counterweight. In the unlikely event that Pakistan acquired nuclear weapons, India would probably be forced to follow suit, for a guarantee by any of the existing nuclear powers would have a very limited application in this case, since India would not necessarily be assured of their political support in a dispute between herself and Pakistan.

There exists, therefore, very little justification for dressing newly emerging nuclear forces within NATO in the garb of potential anti-proliferation devices. Conversely, one would have to regard as exaggerated those predictions which automatically equate the emergence of independent nuclear centres within NATO with global proliferation outside the Atlantic area. In fact, the high price and technological problems experienced by Britain and France cannot but have some deterring effect on outside observers. On the whole, therefore, it is safe to conclude that the existence of the British and French nuclear forces will exert a minimal influence either way on the issue of proliferation beyond the Atlantic region. Proliferation or non-proliferation in the latter areas will be determined by conditions of regional security and super-power guarantees, not by "east of Suez" commitments by either France or Britain.

Seen from the over-all NATO perspective, the existence of independent nuclear weapons in the hands of Britain and France may be credited with having promoted several negative results for the Alliance, such as the failure to reach conventional force goals, and the preoccupation with status and rank stratification, but, so far, hardly with having critically stimulated nuclear proliferation tendencies within NATO.

At present proliferation within NATO seems to have reached a stable plateau. Three allies have achieved nuclear status and an additional three the technological and economic capacity to make the construction of a limited national nuclear force physically feasible. Of the latter three, Canada has rejected it; Italy has not seriously contemplated it; while international treaty commitments, not to mention common sense, have prohibited Germany from making a choice in favour of nuclear weapons.

In 1942 Canada joined the U.S.-U.K. project for developing the atom bomb. By the time the U.S. Atomic Energy Act was passed in 1946, Canada was sufficiently well advanced to have proceeded unilaterally had she chosen to do so. In Canada the matter never even received sufficient consideration to involve a real decision. This not only reflects the strong moral aversion of Canada against nuclear proliferation but also the sound strategic argument that as part of an integrated strategic unit with the United States, Canada, unlike any other NATO ally, is assured of being as effectively shielded by the American strategic deterrent as U.S. territory itself. In future this strategic equality may be disrupted if the U.S. should proceed with installing an ABM system in which Canada was not involved.

Consequently, only a few isolated voices have spoken in favour of an independent Canadian nuclear force. In 1954 Mr. Diefenbaker made a statement to the House of Commons which must seem surprising in view of his later stand as Prime Minister:

> One of the great deterrents to war is atomic power. Its influence for peace may be lost within five years because of our failure to place emphasis on air development and to spend a greater portion of our defence dollar upon aircraft capable of conveying atomic bombs to their destination.[17]

In the late 1950's there were a few supporters for an independent Canadian submarine-based nuclear force in the Canadian military establishment. Intellectual opinion has been conspicuously anti-nuclear, although a few dissenting

[17] Canada, House of Commons, *Debates*, May 20, 1954, p. 4969. Such aircraft might, of course, have remained under dual U.S.-Canadian control.

opinions have been heard. At one time Professor James Eayrs defended the then current view that the deterrent posture of NATO would best be enhanced by convincing the enemy that tactical nuclear weapons would be put to immediate use in a conventional conflict in Europe. Professor Eayrs, furthermore, expressed his opinion in favour of a Canadian nuclear role:

> By producing its own nuclear arsenal, or by insisting upon complete control of that obtained from the United States, the Canadian Government could do much to dispel the public image of the atomic weapon as intrinsically abhorrent and diabolical, qualitatively distinct from weapons which may indeed inflict far greater suffering. It could provide a rare opportunity to instruct Canadians in what, for better or worse, has become a doctrine of the Alliance to which they belong.[18]

Neither strategic arguments nor sentiments in favour of independent nuclear status have survived the agonizing debate under the Diefenbaker Government concerning the nuclear equipment under a "two-key" system of Canada's North American continental air defence squadrons and her forces serving in Europe under NATO assignment.

Theoretically one could argue that the Canadian refusal to exploit its nuclear capability might, by example, also dissuade other countries. Realistically, however, it remains very doubtful whether such an example of abstention does, in fact, exert any meaningful restraint on further proliferation; all the more since Canada, because of its location, commands a unique security position. Its security decisions are therefore less relevant to other countries which occupy a less advantageous strategic position. Furthermore, decisions which affect proliferation are determined more directly by national political and security considerations than by the mere example of other powers. And if examples have any impact, one would gather that the "bad" example of pro-

---

[18] James Eayrs, "Canada, NATO, And the Nth Power Problem", *The Canadian Forum*, XXXIX (April 1959), p. 7. Needless to say, Professor Eayrs no longer holds this view.

liferation rather than the "good" one of abnegation would
be more influential.

As for Italy, many factors tend to make the creation of
an independent nuclear force rather improbable: the limitation of economic resources, the absence of overseas test
sites, the anti-nuclear front of her strong left-wing political
parties, and her meticulous care to avoid a relapse into a
politique de grandeur.[19]

Germany remains the crux of the proliferation problem
in NATO. By the Paris protocols of 1954, the Federal Republic has renounced the right, which other powers may
regard as a birthright accompanying sovereignty, to produce nuclear weapons. While she is not expressly author-
ized to acquire nuclear weapons, there exists no explicit
treaty provision prohibiting such acquisition or their construction on the territory of other powers. But it is realistically inconceivable that her NATO allies or the Soviet
Union would provide Germany with such weapons.[20] Nor
has such a request been made. German opinion has consistently rejected the concept of an independent German nuclear force. A recent sampling of German elite opinion
found that 95 per cent rejected the concept of a national
nuclear force as not being worth its cost, while 90 per cent
expressed general opposition to any form of further proliferation.[21]

[19] Some analysts have expressed concern lest de Gaulle's example
be imitated in Italy. Stanley Hoffmann, in his article, "Europe's Identity Crisis: Between the Past and America", *Daedalus*, Vol. 93, No. 4
(1964), p. 1260, observes that Italy has neither solved her past by
national self-assertion on the Gaullist model, nor by "European" good
behaviour along the German pattern.

[20] As recently as June 21, 1966, Defence Secretary McNamara re-
emphasized that American policy aimed to increase German participation in consultation and planning on nuclear weapons but not to give
Germany control of nuclear weapons, and that the other NATO allies
agreed with this policy. U.S. Senate, Sub-committee on National Security and International Operations of the Committee on Government
Operations, *Hearings* (89th Congress, 2nd Session), p. 208.

[21] Karl Deutsch, "Integration and Arms Control in the European
Political Environment: A Summary Report", *American Political
Science Review*, LX, No. 2 (June 1966), pp. 362-363.

German efforts have aimed in the direction of achieving a preferred position in the process of nuclear planning and consultation, concurrent with an improved status within the Alliance,without striving for actual physical control. Soviet propaganda has skilfully portrayed this as an indication of a German quest for nuclear independence and revanchism. Some similar reservations have been expressed by Germany's own allies. In a speech of November 23, 1964, Prime Minister Wilson voiced his concern lest the American veto over the MLF might in future be converted to a majority decision which could give Germany the opportunity to muster a majority for using the MLF in accordance with German wishes.[22] Unsubstantiated as such concern may be, it has been kept alive by the long reluctance of the German government to divorce itself from the controversial MLF project and the far-reaching demand which the then Foreign Minister, Schröder, made in 1965, when he stated that Germany would make her adherence to a non-proliferation treaty conditional on satisfactory steps toward reunification and an acceptable multilateral nuclear planning solution within NATO.[23]

As for an independent German nuclear force, it would promise to provide a minimum of deterrence at the cost of a

[22] Eugene Hinterhoff, "MLF oder ANF − Zum Problem der Gemeinsamen Streitmacht", *Aussenpolitik*, XVI, No. 3 (March 1965), p. 186.

[23] Foreign Minister Gerhard Schröder, interview with the *Düsseldorfer Nachrichten*, July 3, 1965.

As revealed by Professor Deutsch's above-cited analysis of German opinion, German elite opinion has been consistently less inclined to support the MLF scheme than German government policy would indicate. During the period when the MLF plan received most attention, German elite opinion studies showed only 34 per cent of the latter to be clearly in favour of the MLF and 34 per cent definitely opposed.

"These German elite data", concludes Professor Deutsch (*op, cit.*, p. 363), "tend to disconfirm the notion of a supposedly strong German desire for national nuclear weapons—a desire which would have to be bought off or headed off by offering the German Federal Republic some share in a supranational nuclear weapons system. So far as our evidence goes, there is no such German desire for national nuclear weapons at this time."

maximum destabilization effect in relations with NATO and Eastern Europe. The creation of such a force might tend to promote a redefinition of allied treaty commitments toward Germany that could, among others, take the form of a withdrawal of NATO forces from German territory. Without incurring any additional concrete security gains and without enhancing her bargaining position on the issue of reunification, Germany would thus by her own volition condemn herself to a position of isolation which Soviet diplomacy has so assiduously striven to impose on her.

A EUROPEAN NUCLEAR FORCE

The disadvantages of an integrated European nuclear force would be less obvious than those of separate national nuclear forces. An integrated European nuclear force would constitute a more substantial deterrent than national forces; and it would furthermore eliminate the divisive effect that is created by the perpetuation of the present division into nuclear "haves" and "have-nots" in Europe. National deterrent forces in Europe, as Kurt Birrenbach warns,

> constitute an element of disintegration within Europe . . . . If there are European powers with a special status which qualitatively distinguishes them in a fundamental way from the other member states, the basic idea of a community within Europe will be endangered . . . . There cannot be two different classes of powers within Europe.[24]

In addition to restoring an egalitarian foundation among the European allies, a European nuclear force would, at least theoretically, give them an opportunity to define their particular interests and to defend them, if need be, without American assistance. Some observers have also pointed out that such a force might be expected to give more freedom to U.S. policy outside the NATO area. For under the present conditions, as Philip Mosely points out, Europe remains

²⁴ Kurt Birrenbach, "European Integration and Atlantic Partnership", cited in Karl Cerny and Henry Briefs, *op. cit.*, p. 284.

hostage to the Soviet Union for American "good behaviour" in Asia. An independent European nuclear force would eliminate this hostage relationship, as it would provide the basis for a separate European deterrent, and would consequently allow the United States greater freedom of action in Asia without the restraining impact of the indirect European veto.[25] But to this, one might advance the argument that the complete liberalization of American global policy from European influence might signify a continental rift between the two geographic regions of NATO. A development of this nature would tend to divide NATO, to prompt a reappraisal of U.S. attitudes to Europe, and to act as the prelude for further nuclear proliferation. For this reason several European powers, especially those with particularly intimate relations with the United States, such as Britain and Germany, have categorically opposed the notion of a separate European nuclear force which would operate without direct U.S. participation and veto. French opinion, on the other hand, has generally been favourably inclined toward such a force.

General de Gaulle's habit of portraying the *force de frappe* as a European nuclear deterrent in miniature form, from which all European partners derive distinct security benefits, and as an embryonic European nuclear force, constitutes little more than a piece of rhetoric. For the catastrophic consequences of its use would be such that it is even doubtful whether a French President would resort to this ultimate decision in the defence of his own country. Its use on behalf of another European ally is devoid of credibility. General de Gaulle, as he himself pointed out to Secretary General Stikker,[26] insists on retaining complete freedom to determine the use of the *force de frappe* unimpeded by multiple veto provisions or compulsory consultation procedures. Whatever political realism may be contained in President de Gaulle's grand design for a Europe of father-

[25] *Ibid.*, pp. 261-262.
[26] Dirk Stikker, *op. cit.*, p. 21.

lands, the concept is incompatible with the political and technical demands of a European deterrent force. Only a fully integrated European political unit, with a central executive, could manage the economic burdens of maintaining a meaningful deterrent, and only such an executive group could satisfy the strategic requirements for an immediate nuclear decision, which is mandatory in view of Europe's geographical location and the absence of warning time. Yet it is precisely this concept of an integrated Europe which General de Gaulle finds unacceptable. The paradox of the Gaullist position is best summarized by Paul Reynaud's phrase: "Il a voulu que la France soit à la tête de l'Europe et il n'a pas voulu l'Europe."[27]

No such integrated Europe exists at present, and, from an analysis of present trends and developments, one may doubt the inevitability of its emergence. Perhaps it might be argued, along with Monnet, that by aiming for an independent European nuclear force, a sufficiently powerful catalyst for political integration could be created. Such shotgun tactics, however, seem hardly adequate to perform the process if other inducements have failed. In fact, the very complexity of solving the control problem in a European nuclear force might become the subject of interminable disputes, duplicating at least some of the conflict and ill will which has arisen in conjunction with the control issue in the wider Atlantic setting. The problem of agreeing on a formula for sharing the high costs of developing such a force offers another potential source of conflict among the European members. In consideration of these factors one can hardly escape the impression that the enormous effort of creating an independent European nuclear force might exert a regressive rather than a positive influence on the process of European integration.

Leaving aside the essential precondition of political integration, the realization of a European nuclear force is likely to encounter other severe obstacles. On the financial side, the question is not so much whether Europe possesses adequate means to muster a minimum deterrent force, but whether she is willing to make the necessary sacrifice and whether an acceptable sharing formula could be devised. In her effort to achieve nuclear independence, Europe would not only be forced to divert her financial and material resources to this sector, but she would also continue to be responsible for the major burden of her conventional defence forces, all the more as nuclear independence might bring with it a disengagement of U.S. forces from Europe. The Europeans would be unable to divest themselves of this double burden, for once having provided a nuclear option for themselves, the necessity of retaining a conventional capability in order not to be forced to resort to a nuclear choice would become more pressing than it appears to be at present.

Strategically, Europe also suffers from many inherent disadvantages. Clutched to the bosom of her potential adversary, the peripheral stretch of territory of Western Europe lacks the space for a strategy in depth, for an adequate warning and interception system, and for the dispersal of weapons. Her land-based weapons would be exposed and vulnerable—even hardened bases would be less effective in view of the greater destructive force of Soviet MRBM's which have improved accuracy at shorter distances. Western Europe is furthermore short of unpopulated areas and space for dispersal. Conceivably, the Europeans might focus on developing the kind of weapons system which is most suitable for their particular strategic problems, without necessarily duplicating the kind of system developed by the U.S. for its own needs. Furthermore, the Europeans might station an ICBM force in Greenland or other non-European areas over which they exercised control or with which they could make an agreement of this sort.

A sea-borne second-strike force offers somewhat more positive prospects, especially in view of Europe's access to the Atlantic and North Sea. But such a force has the disadvantage of lower target accuracy and is therefore less well qualified for a counterforce mission. Technical improvements which would give a sea-borne weapons system more accuracy and a higher nuclear payload per missile could overcome this deficiency, but the principal obstacles in the form of high cost and multilateral command and control problems would remain. Furthermore, because of Europe's restricted space and limited resources, it is unlikely that more than one weapons system could be supported simultaneously, and one which would probably be confined to one particular area. The enemy would thus be spared those complicated calculations and uncertainties that arise from being confronted by a variety of weapons systems with a global distribution.

These problems of cost and technology that would arise in the process of constructing and maintaining an independent European nuclear deterrent would be increased substantially if such a deterrent force were also to be equipped with an anti-missile system. Even if the choice were made to "neutralize" a Soviet anti-missile system by means of building more offensive missiles and more sophisticated penetration devices rather than by an independent anti-missile system, the problem of steeply rising costs and increasing technological demands would remain.

In addition, it would require a considerable period of time before an independent European nuclear deterrent could free itself from dependence on U.S. technological assistance, crucial intelligence and targeting information, in addition to communication and warning services. By withholding any of these services the United States could continue to exercise a *de facto* veto over this seemingly independent deterrent. An independent European nuclear force would therefore combine the worst of both worlds: neither independence nor security. The *de facto* veto by the United States would deprive the European nuclear force of the reality of independence, while the shadow of independence and the partial continental divorce between Europe and America would threaten to impair the credibility of the U.S. deterrent as applied to Europe.

AN ATLANTIC "HARDWARE" SOLUTION

The American position on an independent European force has been somewhat ambiguous. President Kennedy in his Grand Design for an American-European partnership, as enunciated in the July 4, 1962, Declaration of Interdependence and his address in Frankfurt's Paulskirche on June 25, 1963, did not explicitly spell out whether the concept of global partnership also included a binuclear sword within the Atlantic area. McGeorge Bundy's address in Copenhagen of September 27, 1962, emphasized that U.S. misgivings about "individual, ineffective, and unintegrated" nuclear forces would not be extended to a European force that was "genuinely unified and multilateral and effectively integrated with our own."[28] At the same time Under-Secretary George Ball reacted favourably to the possibility of creating "a genuinely multilateral medium-range ballistic missile force fully co-ordinated with other deterrent forces of the North Atlantic Treaty Organization."[29] However, neither Bundy's reference to the "integrated" relations between the European and the U.S. nuclear force, nor Ball's concept of a fully "co-ordinated" European force answered the critical question whether the European force was in fact to operate without U.S. membership and the restrictive provision of an American veto.

It seems safe to conclude that these carefully veiled allusions to a European nuclear force were for the most part intended as political hormones that would stimulate the desired growth of European political integration and did not indicate the existence of a clearly conceived strategic plan. All further suggestions for a "hardware" solution to NATO's nuclear dilemma emanating from Washington have re-

[28] McGeorge Bundy, "Building the Atlantic Partnership: Some Lessons from the Past", U.S. Department of State *Bulletin*, XLVII, No. 1217 (Oct. 22, 1962), pp. 604-605.

[29] George W. Ball, "NATO and the Cuban crisis," speech of November 16, 1962, U.S. Department of State, *Bulletin*, XLVII, No. 1223 (December 3, 1962), p. 835.

frained from suggesting a divorce of the U.S. nuclear force from the proposed NATO force. Instead, all concrete proposals have pointed in the direction of an Atlantic nuclear force that provided for American participation and an explicit or implicit veto.

The first specific American offer for the formation of an Atlantic nuclear force was made by the outgoing Eisenhower Administration in December 1960, when Secretary of State Herter informed his NATO colleagues of his government's approval of a NATO-controlled MRBM force for which the U.S. would make available 5 Polaris submarines. The Herter proposal was conditionally tied to a European agreement on the control mechanism and their "purchase from the United States of 100 more medium-range missiles, to be placed on other kinds of ships, under NATO control."[30]

During his visit to Ottawa in May 1961, President Kennedy, in an address to Parliament, expanded the Herter offer into a dual proposal:

> The United States will commit to the NATO command area five—and subsequently still more—Polaris atomic missile submarines, subject to any agreed NATO guidelines on their control and use, and responsive to the needs of all members, but still credible in an emergency. Beyond this we look forward to the possibility of eventually establishing a NATO sea-borne force, which would be truly multilateral in ownership and control, if this should be desired and found feasible by our allies once NATO's non-nuclear goals have been achieved.[31]

The first part of the Kennedy offer was realized at the Athens Conference of 1962, when the United States agreed to "assign" Polaris-armed submarines to NATO. This constituted a psychological gesture that aimed at underlining the credibility of the American nuclear guarantee by allowing other allies to participate through regular NATO channels

---

[30] Robert Osgood, *NATO: The Entangling Alliance* (Chicago: University of Chicago Press, 1962), p. 233.

[31] Cited in the *New York Times*, May 18, 1961.

in planning for the deployment and use of this force. Ownership and actual physical control, however, remained in U.S. hands as before, and the shift of command from the commander of the U.S. Atlantic Fleet to SACLANT, one and the same person serving in a dual capacity, was little more than a bookkeeping entry transferring assets from the accounts of the parent company to the ledger of its subsidiary firm.

Despite these symbolic gestures, the Kennedy Administration remained notably cool to the idea of a multilateral European or Atlantic nuclear force and concentrated its efforts on fortifying Europe's conventional defence. The very fact that this otherwise dynamic and imaginatively versatile Administration left the initiative for solving the multilateral control problem in the hands of its European allies testifies to its notable lack of enthusiasm, if it was not directly intended to serve as a means of manoeuvring the whole issue on to the safe, dead-end road of allied apathy, irresolution and irreconcilability. Under-Secretary Ball prefaced his November 16, 1962 speech on the subject of a multilateral nuclear force by emphasizing that such force was not really needed from a military point of view. In the same vein, Mr. Finletter, the U.S. Ambassador to NATO, dismayed his European colleagues and General Norstad by announcing that it was strategically feasible and preferable to cover all SACEUR's near-tactical nuclear targets by SAC or Polaris missiles from outside the European theatre of operation; consequently, there existed no valid military need for additional missiles in Europe or for the proposed multilateral MRBM force.[32]

The U.S. cancellation of the Skybolt, with its resulting embarrassment to U.S.-British relations, terminated the previous passivity of the Kennedy Administration on this particular issue and produced a major blueprint for a "hard-

[32] Charles Murphy, "NATO at a Nuclear Crossroads", *Fortune* (December 1962), p. 222. Cited in Timothy Stanley, *NATO in Transition: The Future of the Atlantic Alliance* (New York: Praeger, 1965), p. 163.

ware" solution in the form of a multilateral Atlantic nuclear force, the so-called MLF. The Nassau agreement took the form of a two-pronged nuclear solution. The first contingent of this NATO nuclear force was to consist of the British V-bomber force and eventually of Britain's Polaris-armed submarines, to be matched by an equal number of U.S. submarines similarly armed. It was also hoped that it would include the French *force de frappe*, which in turn was to be accorded the long-denied status of equality with the British nuclear force. While these forces were to be assigned to the planning staffs of the Alliance, and subject to directions by NATO, ownership and physical control would remain vested in the donors. A special provision allowed for their withdrawal for exclusively national use in emergency situations.

Insofar as this formula for tripartite nuclear participation excluded those allies that were unable to provide their own nuclear dowry, the Nassau formula, somewhat vaguely, referred to a second contingent in the form of a multilateral NATO force. This aspect of the Nassau agreement constituted the first official endorsement by the United States of the concept of a separate Atlantic multilateral nuclear force and was subsequently spelled out in the form of the MLF proposal.

Whatever the military deterrence qualifications of the MLF, it has not been able to avoid a vocal and printed counterforce bombardment from journalists and military analysts. The vocabulary has ranged from "gimmick" (General Beaufre) and "nonsense" (Field Marshal Lord Montgomery), by way of "political military monstrosity" (Air Marshal Sir John Slessor), to "poor fiction" and "sitting duck" (*Montreal Star*, February 27, 1963). A very lucid analysis of the inception and decline of the MLF idea is found in Professor Kissinger's latest work,[33] and no judicial inquiry into the minute pros and cons is intended here except to examine one principal notion underlying the whole scheme.

Inherent in the ill-fated proposal lay the notion that the

[33] Henry Kissinger, *op. cit.*, pp. 127-159.

nuclear problems of the Alliance could only be resolved by giving members the physical sensation of being able to navigate, touch, press, or paint some aspect or portion, minute as it may be, of an actual nuclear force. This "hardware" concept has been clearly defined by Robert Schaetzel, the former U.S. Deputy Assistant Secretary of State for Atlantic Affairs.

> But whatever is done at this level of cooperation, however valuable it may be, does not get into the labours of producing, operating, and maintaining a nuclear force; indeed in accepting a fair pro rata share of the capital and operating costs of the force. And it is only by getting into these labours—by sharing in ownership and manning of nuclear force—that the non-nuclear countries can be assured that they will, in time of desperate crisis, have a voice in use of the force.[34]

The predicament posed by the "hardware" solution is best exemplified by reconstructing the various considerations which underlay the MLF proposal. The concept of a mixed-manned NATO nuclear force originated in response to the desire to find an alternative to "independent" deterrent forces. This was to be provided by allowing for greater allied participation in the nuclear affairs of the Alliance. This political demand gradually acquired strategic dimensions. A mobile sea-borne force rather than a fixed land-based one seemed preferable since it would create a more equitable distribution of risks among participating allies. Since Germany was unable to provide her own nuclear dowry but was to be accorded a more substantial role in the NATO nuclear planning process, she was to acquire her share of influence through large manpower and financial contributions. Once these political requirements were translated into concrete strategic terms, the final answer took the form of an expensive, mixed-manned, multilateral fleet of

[34] Robert Schaetzel, "The Nuclear Problem and Atlantic Interdependence", *Atlantic Community Quarterly*, I, No. 4 (Winter 1963-64), p. 566.

surface vessels, armed with nuclear MRBM's.[35] In physical terms, the realization of the MLF would have promised to its members participation in the planning and decision-making functions over some 5 per cent of the total nuclear arsenal of the Atlantic powers. But even this fractional force remained subject to a U.S. veto and, what was more discouraging, offered no assurance of a wider spill-over of influence over the remaining 95 per cent.

In the end effect, therefore, this politically tailored solution provided neither a convincing strategic argument nor an acceptable political solution, although the MLF scheme did seriously try to develop a truly Atlantic conception rather than put forward a strictly unilateral U.S. proposal. In the net effect even the description of the MLF as "meaningless but acceptable"[36] turned out to be overly optimistic. What had been intended as a formula for Alliance unity became a blueprint for division which widened the cleavage between Paris and Washington and impaired French-German relations.[37]

In view of these shortcomings, the strong support given to the MLF scheme by the German government seems somewhat surprising, all the more so since the idea was not favoured by the majority of German opinion. But in the opinion of the German government the MLF was not only seen as a means of enhancing German prestige within the Alliance but also as reinsurance against undesired eventualities such as an American disengagement from Europe or an American-Soviet deal which did not take German interests

[35] A senior NATO official in a conversation with this writer enthusiastically defended the MLF idea by saying, in paraphrasing Voltaire, that if the MLF concept did not exist, it would have to be invented. This seems to give a most precise description of the nature of the project. The MLF was not a solution, it was an invention.

[36] *Globe and Mail*, April 18, 1963.

[37] Premier Pompidou warned that any accord between the United States and Germany on the MLF proposal would be incompatible with the French-German Treaty of Co-operation, and would furthermore provoke the U.S.S.R., and hurt the prospects of European unity. (*New York Times*, November 6, 1964)

into account. In addition, Germany might have identified herself with this U.S.-sponsored scheme with the tactical aim of tying her eventual sacrifice of this plan to other political or strategic demands, once the U.S. had disassociated itself from the product of its own creation.

A "hardware" solution, such as the MLF, had the disadvantage of creating an expensive machinery without any substantial gain in available nuclear striking power. Secondly, while it was designed as a countermeasure to nuclear proliferation, it stimulated widespread concern in Eastern Europe, to the *fortissimo obbligato* of Soviet propaganda, and even in the West, that it might serve as the prelude to Germany's nuclear independence. Underlying the MLF concept was the delusive impression that the creation of a nuclear component could somehow resolve what Walt Rostow calls "the whole insoluble theological issue" of multilateral nuclear control. However, neither the MLF, ANF, nor any similar three-letter formula can reconcile "the physical impossibility of combining both trigger and safety catch within a single system comprising two or more equal decision-making entities."[38] A separate NATO nuclear force would not only fail to solve the problem of determining the use or non-use of the American strategic deterrent, but it would tend to intensify the whole problem of nuclear decision-making by creating an additional nuclear force with an unresolved nuclear control problem.

Finally, an MLF type solution would have confined nuclear decision-making functions to the owners and direct participants of this joint nuclear stockholding venture. By making, planning and decision-making functions conditional on ownership and participation in an actual physical nuclear force, a most divisive effect would have been introduced into NATO as a whole, for it would automatically have excluded from this vital business all those allies which for one reason or other refused, or were unable, to exercise their nuclear stockholding option at the inception of this scheme.

[38] Timothy Stanley, *op. cit.*, p. 209.

It would be a matter of sober realism to agree that nuclear planning functions might be more profitably conducted in the intimate atmosphere of a select group than amidst a plenary Alliance forum, and that the critical time element for nuclear decision-making might make mandatory the delegation of decision-making powers to a nuclear executive committee. However, these select groups should operate under the authority and guidelines of the plenary council. Membership in these select groups should be determined on the basis of special qualifications, needs, and expertise, with some opportunity for rotation. The divisive effects on Alliance cohesion that might be generated by forming inner planning staffs and executive decision-making bodies under these precepts would be less serious than if this select membership were to be determined by virtue of nuclear stockholding rights, which, though open to all at the outset, would tend to become crystallized and immutable with time.

VARIATIONS ON THE THEME OF MULTILATERAL CONTROL

Attempts at devising an administrative mechanism that would reconcile the irreconcilable trigger-safety catch dilemma in a multipolar alliance setting have distinguished themselves more by intellectual virtuosity than by practicality. Professor Klaus Knorr, for example, has proposed an intricate manoeuvre for avoiding the paralyzing effect of a *liberum veto* by a so-called *concertina* procedure.[39]

The proposal envisages a multilateral nuclear force that would be protected against unauthorized use by a system of electronic locks rather than through the awkward method of mixed-manning. In a crisis, decision-making powers would devolve from the outer ten to an inner group of four or five members. Decisions could be made by a majority vote of

[39] Klaus Knorr, "A NATO Nuclear Force: The Problem of Management", Princeton University, Center for International Studies, Policy Memorandum, No. 26, 1963.

three. No veto would apply, but those members who disagreed with moving decision-making powers from the outer to the inner group, or who objected to the final decision made by the latter, would be protected by a provision which allowed for their temporary withdrawal from the joint force. They would thereby retain their individual freedom of action without paralyzing the force as a whole.

A solution of this nature, however, seems to lie beyond the sphere of practical management. In the first place, withdrawal by dissenters promises to offer them little protection against the effects of retaliation; it would be difficult to communicate such a last-minute withdrawal to the enemy, and even in the event of successful communication, enemy plans would have been targeted in advance to cover the entire multilateral force and the territory of the participating members. It would therefore be unrealistic to expect the adversary to risk a precipitate alteration in his planned targets in order to exempt dissenters from retaliation. Conversely, any meaningful targeting agreement by this multilateral NATO force would lose its strategic rationale if the contingents of dissenting members could be withdrawn at will.

A variation to this proposal is advanced by David Robison,[40] who suggests a similar *concertina* procedure within the framework of a European nuclear force. The proposal includes an additional provision for the independent use of the national contingents of this collective force, to the effect that "if the European force cannot be activated, any member whose territory or armed forces were attacked by nuclear weapons would be permitted to use the European nuclear weapons entrusted to its military services."[41]

This solution, in fact, seems to promise the worst of both worlds, for it retains the military disadvantages and confusion of the *concertina* withdrawal procedure, while furthering trends toward nuclear proliferation among participants.

[40] David Robison, "A European Co-ordinated Force", *Orbis*, IX, No. 3 (Fall 1965), pp. 656-675.
[41] *Ibid.*, p. 658.

An effective system of multilateral nuclear control provides the rest of the participants with the physical means to block the independent use of any of the national contingents, even if such use should correspond to conditions previously agreed to. Consequently, if the members of this force were to be assured of the unimpaired freedom to use their national contingents in the event of a nuclear attack on their territory, they would in all probability insist on having all physically effective means of multilateral control disbanded in order to prevent a *de facto* veto by their allies. The outcome of this proposal would thus be a set of national nuclear forces operating under European licence.

A conceivable means of reconciling the dilemma between trigger freedom and safety restriction might be found if all opportunity for conscious decision-making during crisis situations were abdicated in favour of an automatic mechanical device. This could be achieved by installing nuclear bomb detection devices which would irrevocably and automatically detonate at the impact of a nuclear attack, or more properly, at the impact of a nuclear explosion on one's territory, for an inadvertent explosion of one's own nuclear weapon would unfortunately prompt the same reaction. But apart from the technological problems of constructing a workable detector and mechanical trigger device, this proposal raises a series of subsidiary problems, such as accidental detonation, enemy acts of sabotage, and tampering efforts by the host country in an effort to convert this automatic mechanism into an independent national nuclear force.[42] Even if an automatic detonator system should offer certain strategic advantages, it is extremely unlikely that

---

[42] As Timothy Stanley points out, (*op. cit.*, p. 209) the acquisition of a nuclear strike force by China adds a new dimension to the problem. For a few Chinese nuclear strikes against Western Europe, once China acquires the capacity for intercontinental delivery, would set into action the automatic detonator device which would be targeted against the Soviet Union. China could thus, with relatively little security risk to herself, precipitate a nuclear war between NATO and the Soviet Union.

nations would voluntarily abdicate to an automatic mechanical device their decision-making power over questions that are vital to their survival.

THE "NON-HARDWARE" OR COMMITTEE APPROACH

Despite the many negative attributes of the MLF "hardware" solution, the abortive scheme may book at least two substantial advantages on its credit side. It represented the first concrete attempt by the United States to engage its allies in the process of nuclear strategic planning and decision-making on a multilateral basis. In the second place, the prolonged period of concentrated study and critical examination of the entire project by a small and informal working group, comprising those countries most interested in eventual MLF membership, has created a useful precedent for continuous strategic planning that is now being perpetuated in the newly formed NATO nuclear planning group.

The work of this special group is centred on the task of extending allied participation to general strategic planning and nuclear information, communication, and decision-making. These goals are to be achieved by relying on existing nuclear forces without the necessity of creating any additional nuclear "hardware". The "non-hardware" solution of extending allied responsibility to matters of nuclear defence may be traced to the 1962 Athens guidelines. At the Athens conference the members of the North Atlantic Alliance agreed on certain general principles relating to the use of nuclear weapons, including the obligation to consult, if at all possible, prior to their use outside the NATO area. At the Athens conference the United States took the unprecedented initiative of making available detailed information regarding the size and location of its nuclear stockpiles in Europe. In addition, it was agreed to continue to share nuclear information, "and to develop procedures, hitherto lacking, for allied consultation on the location and deployment of U.S. nuclear forces in the common defense."[43]

[43] *Ibid.*, p. 202.

Further progress in this direction was made by the NATO ministerial meeting in Ottawa in May 1963, when it was agreed to exchange political and military information more extensively and to make "arrangements for broader participation by officers of NATO member countries in nuclear activities in Allied Command Europe and in coordination of operational planning at Omaha."[44] The latter was to be accomplished by appointing allied liaison officers to Strategic Air Command at Omaha, Nebraska. It is difficult to ascertain whether the role of these liaison officers exceeds that of mere observers and recipients of information, or whether their presence does in fact exert a meaningful influence over SAC's planning functions. Even if the latter has not yet been realized, it remains a desirable goal for future development.

Allied participation in the nuclear activities of SHAPE was to be enhanced by assigning a European officer to the newly created post of nuclear deputy to SACEUR. It is not entirely certain whether the appointment, at least initially, had more than symbolic value in view of the fact that already for some years "the allied commanders of the various regions, together with the allied staff at SHAPE, had developed the nuclear strike program for Allied Command Europe."[45]

The process of extending nuclear information to allies and of broadening allied participation in the formulation of strategy and nuclear planning, along the trend established by the Athens and Ottawa agreements, was temporarily delayed because of the concentrated attention accorded to the MLF "hardware" solution. Now that the MLF and similar

[44] Ottawa Communiqué. Text in the *New York Times*, May 25, 1963.
[45] James E. Moore, "The Military Effectiveness of NATO", in Karl Cerny and Henry Briefs, *op. cit.*, p. 167. The creation of the post of a nuclear deputy may have created rather than solved problems because previously nuclear planning functions were the responsibility of SACEUR's Deputy Chief of Staff for Plans and Operations, who was a German officer, while the new post was filled by a Belgian. Bonn might have regarded this as a demotion rather than an enhancement of its nuclear role.

proposals seem to rest in a state of suspended animation, renewed emphasis has been given to the former trend of gradually increasing allied participation in the management of the existing nuclear force. At the NATO Defence Ministers' meeting in May 1965, Defence Secretary McNamara put forward the proposal for a select committee of Defence Ministers of 4 or 5 allies, charged with the task of developing procedures for improved strategic planning and nuclear consultation in NATO. The suggestion was implemented in November of that year with the creation of an *ad hoc* Select Committee, composed of the defence ministers of 10 allies, and subordinate working groups on information and data exchange, communications and nuclear planning.

During the 1966 Congressional hearings, Defence Secretary McNamara indicated that the planning work of this special committee and its working groups had proved to be of such great use that any MLF or ANF "hardware" solution, if this were still to be considered, could only be "supplementary to, not a substitute for, the organizational structure and procedures necessary to assure greater participation in planning and consultation" in a "pragmatic, realistic, and detailed way."[46]

The MLF proposal has subsequently been filed away quietly, while the "non-hardware" approach has been implemented by the formation of a seven-member permanent nuclear planning group which involves the U.S., Britain, Germany, and Italy as permanent members and three other allies on a rotational basis. At present the rotating seats are occupied by Canada, the Netherlands, and Turkey. The role of the planning group is to improve the allied system of nuclear information and data exchange, to create the basis for an inter-allied crisis communications system, and to formulate guidelines on the use, deployment, or regional withdrawal of nuclear weapons by NATO. At the first ministerial working session of the newly founded group, priority

[46] U.S. Senate, Sub-committee on National Security and International Operations of the Committee on Government Operations, *Hearings*, June 21, 1966 (89th Congress, 2nd Session), pp. 207, 192.

was given to questions relating to the deployment of an ABM system. A more intensive use of the nuclear planning group might also facilitate inter-allied agreement on a nuclear non-proliferation treaty draft and remove at least some of the ground for allied complaints about not being sufficiently consulted on this matter by the United States. In future, this planning group should also direct itself to the question of reducing the stocks of tactical nuclear weapons in the central area of Europe, as part of a gradual disengagement process, and in line with the growing *détente* in Europe and the increasing availability of weapons systems that no longer have to be located in the vulnerable and sensitive central sector in Europe. Even if the planning group should only assist in providing the European allies with a better understanding of the large stockpiles of U.S. nuclear weapons which are available for the defence of Europe, it would serve to overcome one very important reason for their reluctance to agree to a reduction of nuclear weapons in Europe.

The multiple conflicts, paradoxes, and technical dilemmas that are associated with the nuclear control problem in a multinational alliance setting preclude a uniformly satisfactory solution. An adequate solution on the basis of joint staff planning instead of a "hardware" solution has to proceed from the recognition of certain essential prerequisites. These include the establishment of joint planning groups with responsibility for formulating allied strategic concepts and for determining the conditions for the use of nuclear weapons. Apart from the necessity of finding the proper mechanism for intimate, pragmatic, and continuous staff planning, the success of this approach will depend on U.S. willingness to expand the supply of information to its allies and to accept allied representatives on these joint staffs as full-fledged functional members and not merely as representatives tolerated for ceremonial purposes. But even the ceremonial aspect of such allied representation, it must be admitted, is not without substance in overcoming feelings of deprivation, inadequacy, and inferiority among allies and in improving the appearance of allied solidarity and, with it, NATO's deterrent posture.

In addition to widening the basis for allied participation in nuclear planning functions, a solution might eventually have to be found that would allow other NATO allies to share in the economic and scientific "fall-out" benefits from the process of nuclear weapons production by involving them in research and development projects in that particular sector. The decentralization and subcontracting of nuclear research and development projects, however, is not only a matter of utmost technical complexity, but it might once again raise the spectre of nuclear proliferation in Europe, which the entire scheme is meant to counteract. The advanced state of co-operation in research and development of nuclear energy for peaceful purposes that has developed between EURATOM, on the one hand, and the U.S. Atomic Energy Commission and Atomic Energy of Canada Ltd., on the other, may possibly serve as a model for the eventual extension into the field of joint research and development of nuclear weapons, if this should be desired.[47]

A satisfactory realization of these prerequisites would assist in closing the gap between the United States and its allies in information and strategic thinking and thus eliminate a major source of European anxiety and misunderstanding of American strategic motives, which are bound to exist as long as the European allies are merely consumers of U.S.-tailored strategic doctrines. It would, furthermore, provide the NATO allies with the opportunity of exerting a meaningful influence on U.S. strategic decision-making in its formative stage. The decision-making process in the United States stands unrivalled among democratic states for its tortuous complexity, long-windedness, restraining constitutional provisions, and the multiplicity of interplaying interest groups. Consequently, the decision-making process allows for a wide margin of manoeuvrability through its thorough exposure to organized interest groups, including allied

[47] See René Foch, "An Example of Atlantic Partnership: Euratom", *Atlantic Community Quarterly*, II, No. 1 (March 1964), pp. 72-78.

interests, especially if these were to be represented in Washington as part of a regularly constituted strategic planning mechanism. On the other hand, in view of the difficulty of consensus formation in the United States, decisions, once made, tend to assume certain aspects of doctrinaire rigidity and thus give allies only a minimal potential for a subsequent appeal.

The success of allied participation in shaping nuclear policy depends only in part on U.S. willingness to let itself be exposed to allied influence and pressure. It depends equally on allied acceptance of the responsibility that goes with such influence. It would make imperative a more vigorous allied involvement in the complex process of modern strategic analysis than has previously been the case. It might also necessitate their adopting U.S. methods of work and analysis and U.S. idioms, even at the cost of offending national-cultural sensitivities. Most of all, to the participant in the policy-making process influence brings with it at least partial responsibility for the policy outcome. Such responsibility reduces a participant's recourse to other policy options; it limits his freedom to criticize policy; and it impairs his facility to avoid those military commitments or unpleasant political realities and realizations that will emerge from a common policy. The present dilemma in NATO stems precisely from the discrepancy between the allied desire to increase their influence over U.S. policy and their wish to escape from the responsibilities of such influence. The conflict in Viet Nam has increased this dilemma, for the desire of the NATO allies to gain greater influence over American strategic policy is not matched by an equal desire to become more closely associated with U.S. strategic concerns and involvements in Asia.

The active involvement of other NATO members in the formulation of strategy, in planning, and consultation relating to the use of nuclear weapons neither grants them physical control over such weapons, nor does it offer an absolute guarantee that in a crisis the United States would use its strategic forces entirely in accordance with prior common plans and in full harmony with European desires. It would be unrealistic to expect such a rigid guarantee from a superpower with global interests and commitments. The participation of the other allies does, however, represent the best method of communicating on mutual strategic needs and to incorporate these in common defensive plans. Furthermore, the process of multilateral strategic planning and consultation offers the best prospect of "conditioning" the American strategic response to react in the desired and agreed manner.

The ultimate responsibility of physical control cannot but remain in the hands of the President of the United States. Under present strategic conditions the time element has become so critical that a more cumbersome compulsory system of consultation and decision-making would gravely impair the effectiveness of the necessary strategic response in a crisis situation and thereby reduce the credibility of the deterrent. While this might give the impression of unilateral responsibility, it does, in fact, only represent the visible end product of a complex and multi-stage process of prior planning, consultation, and consensus that flows continuously until the ultimate decision. Just as the President acts as his nation's agent in this matter, he also fulfils the function of a trustee of the North Atlantic Alliance. Though committed to consultation and common guidelines, NATO's nuclear trustee must be accorded a degree of freedom of choice and discretion. "Just as a judge has latitude in the interpretation of the law, we should leave our agent some liberty to interpret the circumstances."[48]

This partial assignment of nuclear responsibilities should not become the test case for the conventional observance of the legal norms of constitutional rights and national sovereignty. The delegation of nuclear responsibilities to the President of the United States may be as much in conflict with the constitutional rights of Congress as his nuclear

---

[48] Maurice Faure, Debate at the 1965 NATO Parliamentarians' Conference. Cited in *The Atlantic Community Quarterly*, IV, No. 4 (Winter 1966), p. 474.

trusteeship on behalf of NATO may be said to violate the conventional principles of national sovereignty. Nuclear realities have eroded the traditional concepts of national sovereignty. Under the altered circumstances it might be more realistic to view sovereignty and the unimpeded freedom of national decision-making in the Hegelian context of rational subordination and accommodation to necessity. Sovereignty, according to Stanley Hoffmann's definition, "rather than [being] a reservoir which can only be full or empty, is a divisible nexus of powers of which some may be kept, some limited, some lost."[50]

The reason for centralizing physical control over strategic nuclear weapons may be less compelling when applied to tactical nuclear weapons. The area of operation of the latter is more narrowly confined to a specific region. Operational situations which call for their use may allow more time for consultation and co-ordination among decentralized or regional commands. Furthermore, the immediate impact of the use of tactical nuclear weapons is likely to be less far-reaching than that of strategic nuclear weapons. The resort to tactical nuclear weapons, while critically raising the threshold of escalation, has the advantage of shifting the responsibility for making the ultimate decision onto the shoulders of the adversary. Official Soviet strategy has consistently denied the possibility of keeping a war limited after the engagement of tactical nuclear weapons, and Western strategists attribute extremely high risks to the use of such weapons. There is, however, no *a priori* certainty that immediate strategic retaliation would follow the use of tactical nuclear weapons, and the high probability factor of escalation may under some circumstances be a cardinal inducement for the termination of the conflict, especially if the original *casus belli* was not the result of a deliberately instigated superpower aggression.

[50] Stanley Hoffmann, "International Systems and International Law", in Klaus Knorr and Sidney Verba, eds., *The International System* (Princeton, N.J.: Princeton University Press, 1961), p. 235.

These strategic considerations have given rise to some proposals in favour of European regional command centres with authority over tactical nuclear weapons that would exclude a U.S. veto.

Timothy Stanley's plan provides regional NATO commanders with the right to make autonomous decisions over tactical nuclear weapons for the defence of their particular region in accordance with previously accepted NATO plans. This autonomous decision over tactical nuclear weapons would not be subject to a formal veto, but SACEUR would have to agree that the decision of the regional commander conformed to NATO plans.[51] The proposal again leaves both sides of the trigger-safety catch dilemma unanswered. On the one hand, nuclear proliferation, or at least the appearance of proliferation, would be furthered if smaller allies were given the right to make autonomous decisions over tactical nuclear weapons. On the other hand, SACEUR would still retain a "pocket" veto by the provision which calls for his concurrence. For even if the decision to use tactical nuclear weapons should correspond to NATO military plans, SACEUR could block their use if such a decision were to encounter objections from his own national quarters. An additional veto power would be accorded to the nation which owns these weapons and consequently acts as their custodian. This, in the great majority of cases, would be the United States.

General Norstad has proposed a less decentralized plan for the control of the 5000 or more tactical nuclear weapons that are now available in Europe and integrated into NATO defence plans. According to Norstad,

[51] Timothy Stanley, "Decentralizing Nuclear Control in NATO", *Orbis*, VII, No. 1 (Spring 1963), pp. 46-47. This plan of regional separation does not take into consideration the additional complexities that would arise from a situation as it exists in Germany, where the forces of several allies with a tactical nuclear weapons capability are jointly stationed on the territory of one partner. The immediate concern would thus go beyond the regional NATO commander and the host country.

> most of the NATO nations . . . desire that the authority over the nuclear capability, as well as over the weapons and forces supporting NATO defence plans, should be vested in the Alliance itself. To meet this, the reasonable minimum number of nuclear weapons deployed to support the NATO plans, to give substance to NATO policy, should be wholly committed to the Alliance.[52]

According to the Norstad proposal, the decision to use these nuclear weapons should, if time permits, be made by the NATO Council through a system of weighted voting; otherwise, by the majority vote of an Executive Committee consisting of the heads of government of the United States, Britain, Germany, Italy, and the Secretary General, the latter largely as a representative of the other partners. A niche would be left open for France if she should subsequently desire to associate herself with this group. A dissenting country might withhold its uncommitted national nuclear force components, but "if the dissenting country had made weapons available for use under the common NATO plan, such weapons must remain committed and available."[53] No veto would apply. But in order to avoid proliferation "the actual physical custody of the weapons or warheads should be retained by the country of their origin."[54] Thus the *de facto* veto of the United States as the custodian of these weapons would still remain.

From the point of view of the Alliance the realization of the Norstad Plan with the suspension of the legal right of veto would express U.S. confidence in the behaviour of its allies. It would, furthermore, give statutory form to allied participation in decisions relating to the deployment and use of tactical nuclear weapons. This, however, has already been achieved to a high degree by routine operational practice in NATO commands.

[52] General Lauris Norstad, letter to the Sub-committee on Europe of the Committee on Foreign Affairs, U.S. House of Representatives, *Hearings* (89th Congress, 2nd Session), pp. 223-226.

[53] *Ibid.*, p. 226.

[54] *Ibid.*

But the realization of these plans in relation to tactical nuclear weapons would neither be able to introduce as far-reaching innovations as appear on the surface, nor outflank the remnants of a *de facto* veto. But it would carry with it the spectre of proliferation and might, under certain circumstances, erect a barrier in the continuum between tactical and strategic nuclear weapons. The effectiveness of tactical nuclear weapons depends only in part on their physical impact; to a large extent it depends on the recognized possibility of its "triggering" the U.S. strategic force. The formation of a separate or several separate decision-making centres would be apt to risk an unfortunate rupture in the essential system of graduated continuity. As Defence Secretary McNamara warns,

it would be unwise to divide the nuclear force of NATO into two categories without a proper linkage between them, granting to one group of nations authority to use one category and retaining control of another group of nations or a single nation authority to use the other category. Nuclear war is indivisible.[55]

The paradoxes of nuclear management in a multilateral setting preclude a clear-cut and unassailable settlement. It is not a fruitful vineyard for perfectionists. A solution to the problem will inevitably produce diffuse and amorphous characteristics. Residual elements of doubt and uncertainty can only be bridged in a spirit of trust and perceived common interests. A settlement of the nuclear control problem in NATO is more likely to be reached by accommodation and a compromise formula than by a precise mathematical solution. At the moment the recently created nuclear planning group represents an experiment rather than a settlement of the problem. Only success in its actual implementation will prove whether it constitutes an acceptable solution.

[55] Robert McNamara, testimony before the U.S. Senate, Sub-committee on National Security and International Operations of the Committee on Government Operations (89th Congress, 2nd Session), p. 206.

4

The Challenge to Military
Integration in NATO

THE ESTABLISHMENT of an integrated system of defence in
the central sector of Europe must be regarded as one of
NATO's most significant achievements and as an innovation
in peacetime alliance behaviour.

Like the question of nuclear policy in NATO, the issue
of military integration involves both political and military
aspects. On the whole, military integration has proceeded so
successfully that it has not presented a major controversy
until the recent French policy of challenging both the
principle and practice of integration. The concept of integration combines two basic considerations. First, it involves
the traditional mechanism of providing for a system of collective defence against the threat of a superior force. Secondly, it is based on the realization that conditions of modern warfare make a post-attack collective defence arrangement a highly inadequate instrument for security. Historically, whatever integration of allied forces under one central
command was achieved had to await the actual event of
hostilities. Thus it was only toward the end of World War I
that a joint allied military command was formed; in World

War II the creation of a Combined Chiefs of Staff was postponed until U.S. entry into the war and never included the Soviet Union.

The peacetime military integration which has developed in NATO practice offers at least a three-fold advantage over the traditional procedure: it copes with the *Blitzkrieg* characteristics of modern conventional warfare by preparing a defensive infrastructure for an immediate joint response; it creates a system of joint sharing in the burdens and management of defence; and it provides a framework that makes the continued presence of "guest" forces on the territory of certain allies politically acceptable.

Peacetime military integration in NATO extends to operational planning on forces and weapons, including tactical nuclear weapons, that have been "assigned" to Europe. On a *de facto* basis it also includes the joint management of supplies, communications, and the air warning system in that sector. In peacetime, integration does not involve the exercise of command functions, except with relation to German troops and in the case of NATO manoeuvres. Even in the event of conflict, the final responsibility for recruiting, supplying, and equipping of forces remains in the hands of the respective national governments, just as the actual battlefield command over the fighting units will be exercised by officers representing the same nationality as their troops. No mixed manning is envisaged.

Military integration as practised in NATO is not supranationalism. It represents a form of intensified allied cooperation rather than a rigid system of individual national subordination. The real achievement in NATO's military integration has been the creation of a collective apparatus and a set of common plans which can rapidly be put into operation in the event of conflict. Moreover, peacetime integration has been responsible for inculcating habits and practices of interdependence among a large sector of the military elite of NATO members and has thus laid the intellectual and psychological basis for effective co-coperation and joint decision-making in wartime.

Integration stresses allied interdependence and gives visible form to U.S. involvement in the defence of Europe and thus improves the allied deterrent. Integration also acts as the instrument for the accommodation and absorption of U.S. troops into the fabric of European life, without producing the political and psychological strains that might accompany their presence on a purely bilateral basis.

In addition, integration was regarded as the best means to commit the United States to the defence of Europe and to prevent a relapse into a policy of isolationism. Integration was considered "a political necessity because of the vagueness of the terms of the treaty,"[1] and, ironical as this may seem today, found its strongest champion in France. Now, after two decades of active U.S. involvement in Europe, there exists little fear of a termination of American interest in Europe, including the interest to defend Europe. This being the case, Europeans seem to desire a little more U.S. detachment from the general affairs of Europe rather than increased integration. Firm assurance, rather than doubt, of the continued American interest in the defence of Europe allows France the luxury to disagree with U.S. policy and to advocate a reduced American role in Europe.

Originally military integration also played an intra-Alliance "controlling" role in relation to Germany. Integration promised to minimize the contingency of an unsanctioned unilateral military move by Germany, as it tied the German defence not only to the presence of other allied forces on its territory, but also to common operational plans, a joint allied command structure, and allied logistic support. Such thinking today would be entirely inappropriate. In the long run an alliance cannot exist if one of its principal purposes is to use its physical resources to restrain one of its principal participants. The "control" functions which now exist in relation to Germany operate in a more indirect manner. In the first place, the practice of joint planning and continuous

[1] André Beaufre, *NATO and Europe* (New York: Alfred Knopf, 1966), p. 28.

consultation inculcates in members a greater consciousness of allied needs and promotes mutual responsiveness in place of a strictly unilateral national approach. Secondly, the incentive for independent military adventures is controlled as allies derive a feeling of security from their active engagement in the planning functions of the Alliance. Germany's central position in Europe, and the concentration of Soviet and other Communist allied forces on her boundaries, make her strategically the most vulnerable of the NATO allies, just as her division makes her the politically most exposed member of the Alliance. If the French tendency to veer toward unrestrained unilateralism stems from a sense of relative security, Germany might proceed to search for a more independent status, not because of an awakened "profile neurosis" but from a sense of chronic insecurity. If, on the other hand, NATO were to identify itself with Germany's security needs by providing a meaningful German role in the military planning functions of the Alliance, including participation in nuclear planning, NATO would furnish the best guarantee against the resurgence of a German national separatism in her foreign and military policy. NATO's inherent "control" functions can thus promote political stabilization and nuclear non-proliferation.

Insofar as Soviet hostility toward NATO is unabated, one must conclude that NATO's potential for control, especially with reference to Germany, is either being ignored by the Kremlin, or regarded as less valuable than the propagandistic gains of a continued and relentless anti-NATO front. Moscow has refused to accept the "controlling" influence which NATO has on Germany and has held the organization responsible for promoting an allegedly renascent policy of German militarism and revanchism.

It is interesting to note, however, that certain voices in other East European countries have been less critical of NATO. Some Polish writers have recently criticized General de Gaulle's aim of eliminating super-power involvement in

Europe, a policy which was judged to be detrimental to East European security.[2]

RATIONALE AND IMPACT OF THE FRENCH WITHDRAWAL

As of July 1, 1966, France's withdrawal from the integrated defence system of NATO has become a *fait accompli.*

The overriding rationale of the French position seems to be derived from the Gaullist conception of national sovereignty, which equates integration with subordination and views the "permanent presence of allied military elements" in France and the "continued use made of her skies" as an infringement of the full exercise of French sovereignty which she is determined to recover.[3] It is the aim of Gaullist policy once more to harmonize the reality of international relations today with the rigid legal doctrine of sovereignty, as it evolved in the 18th and 19th centuries in accordance with political and technological conditions then existing.

As a partial reflection of his own personal dynamism and heroic leadership, General de Gaulle's conception of the management of international affairs resembles the highly personality-oriented and, by modern standards, somewhat dilettantish and improvised nature of 18th century states-

[2] Edmund Osmanczyk, "Zjednoczona Europa, Zjednoczone Niemcy, i co dalej?", *Polityka*, May 5, 1965; and Ludwik Debinski, "Polska, Francja, Niemcy", *Tygodnik Powszechny*, August 29, 1965. Both cited in Adam Bromke, "Poland and France: The Sentimental Friendship", *East Europe*, XV, No. 2 (February 1966), p. 13. Important as this may be as an indication of altered opinion, it must be accepted as a minority sentiment, for Poland's Foreign Minister, Adam Rapacki, in his article, "The Polish Plan for a Nuclear-Free Zone Today", *International Affairs*, Vol. 39 (January 1963), p. 8, insists that his country has "never been convinced by assertions that the fact of Western Germany's membership of NATO, of the Common Market, and of all sorts of forms of so-called Western Union has constituted the best guarantee of a peaceful policy by that state."

[3] Unofficial translation of General de Gaulle's letter to President Johnson, March 7, 1966. Cited in the *New York Times*, March 25, 1966.

manship. It shuns the impersonal rule of technocratic bodies, supranational agencies, and integrated military staffs, as well as the unruly and open international forum of quasi-parliamentary assemblies such as the UN. His preference lies with intimate directorates of heads of government of major powers or their representatives: the authority of the Five in the Security Council rather than the rule of the General Assembly; a triumvirate of Britain, France, and the United States in NATO, in place of the integrated planning staffs of SHAPE and the more representative forum of the NATO Council; and a duumvirate of French-German cooperation and leadership in the Europe of the Six in place of the partially supranational European Commission. In his television address of December 31, 1964, President de Gaulle underlined his country's willingness to continue to cooperate with its allies but vowed to restore French independence in matters relating to her economy, currency, defence, and foreign policy. At the same time he rejected any system of integration, supranationalism, and Atlanticism which would perpetuate American hegemony over Europe.[4]

General de Gaulle's firm stand against military integration is also reinforced by his belief that integration tends to freeze the *status quo* in Europe and thus impairs the prospects of a settlement between Eastern and Western Europe. Underlying this is General de Gaulle's outright dismissal of the threat of a conventional conflict in Europe. This is an assumption which has validity with respect to the threat of a premeditated and deliberately executed Soviet aggression with massive conventional forces, but it dismisses a whole range of conventional conflict contingencies that might arise from other situations. Or it may be that France already regards the German conventional forces as large enough to form a deterring threshold against a large-scale conventional attack and as sufficient to cope with minor incidents and probing actions singly and without need of an allied

[4] Cited in Carl Ehrhardt, "De Gaulle und die Integrationsidee", *Aussenpolitik*, XVI, No. 12 (December 1965), p. 807.

integrated defence system. But if this were the case, it is hardly a matter to which French prestige-oriented policy would give open recognition.

Finally, the French action reflects the dissatisfaction of its present government with the strategy of flexible response which cannot be effectively exercised at all levels without resorting to some form of military integration. According to the French position, integration of conventional forces in Europe is regarded as unnecessary in view of the supposedly non-existent threat of conventional conflict, and undesirable insofar as it weakens the credibility of massive retaliation by the U.S. According to French claims, the *force de frappe* provides a substitute for Europe's former dependence on conventional defence. Ostensibly, this position emphasizes French independence from the United States, but in reality it seeks to deprive Washington of the option of defending Europe by other than nuclear means. To acknowledge this openly would constitute recognition of continued European dependence on the United States which General de Gaule naturally wishes to avoid. The *force de frappe*, therefore, provides a rhetorical fig-leaf to cloak the nudity of the dilemma.

The following immediate or short-term developments have resulted from the French decision to withdraw from the integrated military structure of NATO:

1) French withdrawal from the integrated military staffs of SHAPE and AFCENT (Allied Forces Central Europe) on July 1, 1966. Withdrawal from the Mediterranean Command, SACLANT, and the Channel Command had already taken place prior to the last action.

2) The eviction of these integrated NATO organizations and of the U.S. European Command Headquarters from French soil.

3) The removal from French territory of 2 U.S. C-130 transport squadrons, 6 U.S. reconnaissance squadrons, the 322nd U.S. Air Division Headquarters at Châteauroux, 2 Canadian CF-104 reconnaissance squadrons, and of the Canadian Air Division Headquarters at Metz.

4) The removal of all supply bases and communication installations under U.S. command. These had been established by bilateral French-U.S. agreements within the general framework of NATO defence. The eviction notice affects some 33,000 military and 2,000 civilian personnel of the U.S.[5] and some 2,000 Canadian military personnel.[6] The eviction date for all categories (other than 1) was April 1, 1967.

5) The withdrawal from NATO command of some 65,000 French ground forces and 4,000 airmen stationed in Germany. However, following a provisional accord in July and a formal French-German bilateral agreement of December 1966, it has been decided that approximately some 62,000 French troops will remain in the Federal Republic under direct French national rather than NATO command.[7]

The more far-reaching political and military consequences of the French action are extremely difficult to predict, as they largely depend on a clarification of long-term French aims and the willingness and ability of the other allies to cope with the new situation.

However successful the accommodation efforts, and even if France should choose to co-operate from the outside with the integrated military structure of NATO, there can be no doubt that the French move has introduced very considerable military liabilities. A conventional defence of Western Europe has always been handicapped by its peripheral geographic position which allows for little warning time, dispersal space, manoeuvrability, and rear bases. The loss of French territory in the very heart of Western Europe must therefore be felt most keenly. Headquarters, bases, and supply lines may, at great cost and with extra effort, be relocated in Britain, the Benelux countries, or Germany. This is now being undertaken. However, in their new location these installations will be more crowded, more vulnerable, and more restricted in the range of operational options. Moreover, with the loss of France from the integrated

[5] *New York Times*, April 9, 1966.
[6] *Globe and Mail*, March 12, 1966.
[7] *New York Times*, December 22, 1966.

NATO command, the territorial linchpin between the central and southern sector of Europe will be lost. The result may well be a move in the direction of greater regional division and autonomy in the NATO command structure and its crystallization into two essentially separate regional groupings in Europe, involving a northern tier with Britain, Germany, the Benelux and Scandinavian members, together with the two North American members; and a southern tier composed of Italy, Greece, Turkey, Portugal, together with the U.S. and possibly Great Britain.

Certain ameliorating factors, however, should not be overlooked in reassessing the new situation. The inclusion of Spain, as compensation for the partial loss of France, has been considered. But apart from the political repercussions of such a move, the use of Spanish territory for air and supply bases would be of little significance if Spain were to be isolated as the result of France's absence. "The importance of France", according to Dean Acheson, "is where France is, and if France is out of the organization, then Spain is separated from the rest of NATO and cannot play any particularly important part."[8] On the other hand, it must be realized that after Germany's rearmament and the increase of conventional forces in Europe, the present NATO strategy of forward defence relies on a defence effort on German soil and does not envisage French territory as the actual field of battle in the case of a conventional engagement, other than relying on it for bases and supply depots. A conflict in which enemy ground forces had successfully penetrated as far as France would no longer be within the confines of conventional warfare. Also technological advances in the field of long-range air transport, tactical support aircraft of intercontinental range, and the use of the F-111 for strike missions will make possible the sectoral reinforcement with troops and supplies, as well as ground support and strike reconnaissance roles, that can use the rear bases of the

[8] Dean Acheson, *The Crisis in NATO*, Hearings before the Subcommittee on Europe of the House Foreign Affairs Committee, U.S. House of Representatives (89th Congress, 2nd Session), p. 181.

North American hinterland rather than rely exclusively on the forward area of Europe.

The principal shock absorber of the French withdrawal would be France's own willingness to continue co-operation from outside the integrated defence system. If the aim of the French action were to find a formal escape from the appearance of subordination under an integrated defence system, such co-operation could, indeed, assume a militarily meaningful level which would forfeit relatively few benefits of integration. A bilateral agreement regulating the continued presence of French forces in Germany has already been concluded. This could assume greater proportions than merely acting as an olive branch for Germany. As long as the central apparatus of military integration remains intact, the military presence of French troops in Germany might provide the means for France's indirect participation and close liaison with the NATO staffs, with the possibility of rapid reintegration, at least of ground forces, in the event of crisis. If France demonstrates the will for co-operation, and the other allies for accommodation, a solution acceptable to NATO as a whole might be found with respect to bases and supply lines on French territory, possibly by entrusting their management to French civilian authorities. Whatever its general concern for the effectiveness of the NATO defence posture, the French government cannot remain oblivious to its dependence on the forward space and the early warning facilities of its NATO allies in order to retain any operational capability for its own *force de frappe*. Access to the integrated warning system, as Premier Pompidou has indicated, is a matter of importance to France and would "be an issue for negotiation", and hopefully, one for agreement.[9] Thus French dependence on forward space and warning facilities, and the requirement of the other allies for bases and supply lines in the rear area, might provide a comple-

[9] Premier Pompidou's address to the French National Assembly, April 20, 1966. Cited in the *New York Times*, April 21, 1966.

mentary *quid pro quo* in negotiating a tolerable arrangement for the Alliance. In the Brussels communiqué of June 1966, it was agreed to hold discussions with the aim of reaching agreement with France on the latter's participation in NADGE and other NATO infrastructure projects.

At this stage is seems quite possible that an acceptable agreement will be reached whereby the pipeline system on French territory would be unilaterally operated by France but available for allied use. Another approach, namely the relocation of the pipeline system, is also being contemplated. In the same way France is likely to co-operate in making its communication facilities available to the Alliance. In addition, the U.S. has offered the use of its military satellite communications system to its European allies "and to collaborate in the joint development of a new system specifically for the Alliance."[10] Access to the U.S. military satellite communications system will reduce allied dependence on the communications facilities which are located on French soil. So far France has continued to grant overflight privileges to allied aircraft, permission being granted on a monthly basis instead of the previous annual arrangement. Furthermore, France is still involved in the allied air defence warning system, part of which runs through the eastern part of her territory.

In all likelihood, however, final agreement will be reached at less than the optimum level portrayed above. France's extreme sensitivity, or "profile neurosis", about retaining the fullest measure of independence and sovereignty imposes severe burdens on the process of practical settlement. Apart from the French concern for sovereignty, its objection to military integration must, in part at least, be attributed either to a different interpretation of the nature of the threat from that held by the majority of the other allies, or to a different conception of the nature and demands of modern warfare. Such basic differences on stra-

---

[10] *New York Times*, September 29, 1966.

tegic interpretations would tend to minimize the possibility of an optimum solution to the present problem.

The unilateral *fait accompli* without prior consultation, which proceeded from the assumption that negotiations could not lead to a mutually acceptable result, not only contradicted the spirit of the Alliance, and the letter of the Franco-German Treaty of Mutual Co-operation, but also set an unfortunate precedent for future Alliance behaviour. It also unnecessarily mortgaged the prospects for an acceptable accommodation. The style of the French action and the uncompromising rejection of the principle of military integration, which enjoys particularly strong support among the ranks of the smaller allies, had the unfortunate result of pitting them against France despite their sympathy for many of General de Gaulle's aspirations. The result, at least temporarily, has been a reduction of the smaller members' facility for mediation.

From the point of view of the Alliance the worst possible consequence of the French action would arise from a situation where France's policy aims were motivated not merely by the desire to recover lost sovereignty and to broaden her manoeuvrability, but represented a conscious cultivation of the option of neutrality in the event of renewed conflict in Europe. In the present French-U.S. discussions regarding the military facilities on French soil that might be put at the disposal of the U.S. in the event of a European conflict, the French government has been careful to indicate that such co-operation would be restricted to those circumstances in which both should find themselves engaged in a European conflict situation. This position seems to imply that such joint engagement cannot be taken for granted. From this one would gain the impression that the French government deliberately seeks to preserve its option of neutrality in case of a European conflict and thus to give a more flexible interpretation to the NATO Treaty than was originally envisaged when it was agreed that an attack on one was automatically to be treated as an attack against all.

As the result of the deterioration of the integrated defence system in Europe, other allies, and especially Germany, might feel forced to seek compensation for their security loss by cultivating closer relations with the U.S. on a strictly bilateral basis. The U.S. might reciprocate in this trend because of its increased dependence on the military role of Germany. But any deliberate attempt to duplicate a possible trend toward greater military bilateralism by political measures that would seek to transform NATO into a Bonn-Washington axis, to isolate France and to place her in some form of political quarantine, would have most unfortunate political consequences. Not only France, but also the other West and East European powers, would regard with great suspicion a U.S.-German bridgehead that was not moored to a more solid collective European foundation. Any conscious efforts to isolate France in Europe might be countered by a reorientation of France's present East European policy, including a non-aggression pact with the U.S.S.R. and recognition of East Germany, which in turn would be highly disturbing to Germany and to German-French relations.

It must also be realized that from whatever perspective one might want to look at it—geographic, strategic, or cultural—France remains the key to any further integration in Europe and to a multilateral involvement with Eastern Europe. Both Britain and Germany could play a major role in this integrative process, but neither by itself could be the principal agent. Culturally, both Britain and Germany are more peripheral than France in the sense that they do not possess the same level of integrative cultural affinity to as many different European nations as does France. Secondly, both Britain and Germany suffer from historical liabilities which promise to continue in some form even in the context of an integrated Europe. With respect to Britain, what is involved is her traditional aloofness from European affairs, which might continue to find expression in special bilateral ties and commitments to outside regions which the other

European members would not share. In the case of Germany, it is the historical problem of reconciling Germany's extraordinary resources and dynamism with intra-European security considerations. The problem continues as the result of Germany's natural quest for reunification.

Therefore, as long as France continues to hold the key that might either open the passage for further European integration—expansion could proceed both sectorally or geographically—or veto such progress, a combined German-American policy which seeks to isolate France from the rest of Europe would have the boomerang effect of isolating Germany from Western Europe and of impairing a German *rapprochement* with Eastern Europe.

Since the French position on military integration seems irrevocable, NATO efforts must be directed at maximizing co-operation with France, while the latter remains outside the integrated system. In addition, it will be necessary to consider necessary changes in the present integrated defence structure in order to accommodate other allies more successfully than has been possible with France.

One of the principal objections which President de Gaulle has raised against the practice of military integration in NATO was that it constituted a direct form of European subordination to the U.S. In his press conference of September 9, 1965, General de Gaulle declared that no later than 1969 France would terminate her subordination to a foreign power, which according to NATO usage was euphemistically referred to as integration.[11]

If this criticism refers to the entire principle of integration, then nothing short of total abolition of the system would be satisfactory. If, however, as seems to be the case with most of the other European allies, criticism is with the practical implementation and not with the principle of integration, then measures for improving the situation may be contemplated.

[11] Cited in *Europa-Archiv*, XX, No. 19 (Oct. 1965) p. D 493.

In the first place, it will be necessary to examine how NATO's cumbersomely large and overly complex central and regional command structure in Europe—more a result of political compromise than of military logic—could be simplified, especially in view of improved communications facilities.[12]

Another approach, in the form of allotting more of the top positions at SHAPE and other regional European commands to officers of the European allies, has been a frequently suggested remedy which would represent both a functional and a symbolic gain for the Europeans. The present trend has already been in this direction. This has been particularly noticeable in the field of tactical nuclear weapons planning, which formerly represented a preserve "For American Eyes Only" but now involves senior officers of other allies.

Ultimately, the logical conclusion to this trend would be the appointment of a European as SACEUR. This might eventually become practical if, after considerable progress in the East-West *détente* in Europe, both sides were to regard Europe as a sanctuary and symbol of their co-operative intentions. Under those conditions Europeans might feel sufficiently secure to accept a formal U.S. guarantee without

---

[12] General Beaufre (*NATO and Europe*, pp. 138-140) proposes to eliminate most of NATO's regional commands and to organize the defence of the European allies on the basis of national commands under the central direction of a Supreme Allied Commander Europe. It is questionable whether such a national-oriented defence, even with the best of co-operation, would be able to integrate for the task of jointly managing Europe's air defence and warning system, which could not be conducted on a purely national level. The proposal, furthermore, raises some far-reaching political issues, for it would lead to the formation of an independent German command and general staff; moreover, "guest" forces would be placed under German command. The present French government would be the last to accept such a condition for stationing its forces in Germany. Also the idea of Germans commanding U.S. forces, even if the latter were to retain direct physical custody over tactical nuclear weapons, would be detrimental to the prospects of *détente* in Europe.

need of supporting evidence in the form of a physical presence of U.S. troops in Europe.[13]

At the present stage, however, certain considerations would argue very strongly against the immediate "Europeanization" of SACEUR.

In the first place, if actually confronted with the choice of naming one from their own ranks, the European allies would probably experience great difficulty in agreeing. Given the present level of political integration in Europe, the choice of an American officer, who represents a country which is removed from Europe, not only geographically but also in terms of the category of power which it occupies, still seems to be less divisive and less likely to cause a European tug-of-war over rank and prestige, than would the appointment of a European officer. This is somewhat analogous to the situation confronting the OAS, where Latin American members have for long been critical about the fact that the seat of the Organization is in Washington; yet rank and prestige questions have prevented agreement among them about its relocation. The choice of a European officer to SACEUR would, furthermore, be made more controversial by the fact that the logical successor to an American officer would be an officer representing Western Europe's most powerful military establishment, Germany.

Secondly, as long as NATO is committed to a strategy of flexible response and regards the presence of U.S. forces in Europe as an integral part of the American nuclear guarantee, it seems essential that the most direct and uninterrupted links be maintained between Europe's conventional defence forces and the American nuclear arsenal. This link is enhanced if SACEUR is the immediate representative of the U.S. President with direct access to him. It is unlikely that a European officer could establish the same immediate access and exercise the same degree of persuasive influence over the President as would an American officer.

[13] Under those circumstances, Europeans might be willing to dispense with an integrated defence system altogether, and thus the question of the nationality of SACEUR would become irrelevant.

Two other factors need to be considered in this context. The U.S. is unlikely to augment the conventional defence of Europe with its nuclear commitment, if it should be deprived of the over-all direction of military operations that might involve the decision to resort to nuclear weapons. Secondly, the reduced fighting strength and a possible deterrence gap that might arise from the gradual reduction of U.S. forces in Europe could be augmented by American-based air-mobile defence units that could be deployed in Europe in case of emergency. The direction of this intercontinental mobile operation and its rapid integration into the European defence structure, as well as the credibility of its use, would all be aided if the position of SACEUR were filled by a U.S. officer with direct access to the top U.S. military establishment and the President.

It seems that the basic problem arising from NATO's integrated defence system is more one of function than of representation and should be approached in this manner. As originally envisaged, the role of SACEUR was that of military commander over NATO's forces in Europe. But as the result of the shortcomings of the Standing Group and the Military Committee in formulating NATO's military plans and strategic doctrines, SACEUR has assumed an extraordinarily important role with respect to these latter functions. Among these has been the role of defining the strategic needs of the European allies and of proposing measures that would meet these. While it cannot be doubted that past incumbents of the calibre of General Norstad "represented" the interests of the European allies very effectively, it must be realized that in the long run such tutelage is unacceptable to the European members. Europeans must assume the responsibility and must find the means to define and coordinate their own strategic interests. This, as was indicated, need not take the form (nor would it be resolved by such measure) of appointing a European officer to the post of SACEUR. What is required, however, is some return to the original intention of NATO, where SACEUR's military command and routine administrative duties would be divorced from the more far-reaching strategic planning functions of the Alliance.[14]

With closer European economic integration and political consensus, the European allies should be able to assume a more effective role in the strategic planning functions of the Alliance, either by constituting a more solid European bloc in the Military Committee, or by acting through a strengthened WEU forum, or through a combination of both. In the same way, on questions of nuclear policy the European members could enhance their position by providing a corporate European stand in the newly constituted nuclear planning committee. These measures would promise the best opportunity of retaining the fundamentals of allied integration, as long as this remains militarily and politically desirable, while facilitating the emergence of a more corporate European approach in defining and organizing its security interests.

[14] On the other hand, one cannot ignore the argument that SACEUR, who is in more direct contact with and more immediately dependent on the military forces of his allies than is true for a planning group, has shown himself more responsive and sympathetic to the views of the smaller allies than the Standing Group or other NATO military planning bodies.

5
NATO and the Smaller Members

THE POWER discrepancies among the members of the North Atlantic Alliance have created a stratification in terms of power as intricate as that of the *Almanach de Gotha*. To some extent all NATO allies except the U.S. super-power share the attribute of being small powers. But if one takes a micro-survey of intra-alliance power relationships, allies such as Britain and France, because of their position as former "great powers", nuclear status, and more than strictly regional military commitments, and Germany, as the most important military power in Western Europe, stand out from such "middle" powers as Canada, Italy, and Turkey. In turn, the latter possess a different power base than NATO's small powers such as the Benelux and Scandinavian members, Greece, Iceland, and Portugal.

The different smaller members of NATO, that is those which in terms of power may be classified as small or "middle" powers, are by no means of uniform importance to the Alliance and do not necessarily follow complementary policies and goals. The strategic importance of the Benelux countries, an importance which has recently increased as

the result of France's withdrawal from the integrated defence system in Europe, is quite out of proportion to the size
of their territory and forces. There also exists a wide range
of different policy goals among smaller allies. As a North
American country with close European ties, Canada has
been particularly concerned with strengthening the community of interests between Europe and North America
and, partly as the consequence of domestic political considerations, with maintaining close co-operation with France.
With regards to NATO membership, Portugal's policy must
largely be seen as following the goal of increasing her share
of military assistance from the Alliance, of legitimizing her
régime by this close international association with a group
of powers, and, if not of enlisting support, at least of deterring active allied interference in her colonial policy.

Despite this range in power, importance, and policy
goals, the smaller NATO allies have revealed common features in their attitudes, demands, and reservations. These
common features are particularly pronounced in the smaller
powers' preference for multilateral rather than strictly bilateral relations in dealing with the United States. The same
tendency is occasionally even manifested in their relations
with other major allies, as for example in Danish-German
relations. The smaller members have also been aligned on
the issue of supporting the principle and practice of improved consultation. Since they frequently take a more regional orientation than the major allies, they have been
averse to any geographic extension of their commitments under the North Atlantic Treaty. This combination of maximum consultation, on the one hand, and minimum commitments, on the other, has frequently involved the smaller
members in a conflict of aims, if increased consultation ap-
peared to be the first step toward increased responsibilities
and commitments.

The strategic requirements of the missile age have rendered the great powers less dependent on the smaller allies
for military bases and facilities. While the latter continue to
rely on the Alliance for their security, the security of the

major allies seems to have become markedly less dependent on whatever contributions the smaller can make. The question therefore arises whether the smaller members have become mere consumers rather than producers or participants of security. If that were indeed the case, then "the imbalance between the needs of the great powers and the small ones is likely to be harmful to both in the long run."[1]

During the period when the intercontinental bomber constituted almost the sole nuclear threat to the United States, accessibility to Canadian territory in the form of overflight privileges and forward radar and weather stations on Canadian territory contributed significantly to determine the credibility or non-credibility of the American retaliatory force. Canada's principal military contribution to NATO during that particular strategic phase was thus in the Arctic wastelands rather than in the lowlands of Westphalia. The gradual diminution of the bomber threat entails a comparable reduction in the strategic value of several of the smaller allies. However, the decline of the strategic bomber threat itself will become a reality only if the forward warning facilities remain intact, or are replaced by comparable installations in outer space. The manned bomber offers certain inherent strategic advantages over missiles in terms of greater flexibility, accuracy, and destructive power. Without the existence of adequate warning facilities the manned bomber would add to these inherent advantages also the key factor of low vulnerability, which at present accounts for the superiority of the missile over the bomber. One could even speculate that the installation of an ABM system might renew interest in the manned bomber, as it would render missiles less effective.

From these existing strategic conditions one may conclude that the U.S. still retains considerable interest in the bomber and missile warning and communications facilities on the territory of its NATO allies. Even with respect to the

[1] Nils Orvik, "NATO: The Role of the Small Members", *International Journal*, XXI, No. 2 (Spring 1966), p. 177.

missile threat, U.S. interest in access to Canadian territory and facilities would again increase if, in the event of a decision to install an anti-missile system, the United States were to adopt a more extensive system that covered a whole area, instead of the more restricted target or terminal-point type of ABM system, which so far has received most attention.

The major allies' dependence on the security of their smaller partners is a more binding factor in preserving Alliance cohesion than the purely military utility of the reciprocal services which the latter can render. As recipients of the nuclear guarantee of the super-power, and, with the exception of Canada, formerly also of direct economic and military aid, the smaller allies may be regarded as consumers of security, but only in the material sense, for NATO serves as the means of arranging for the forward defence of the major powers by facilitating the conventional defence of the smaller allies and by including them in the orbit of deterrence. Neither the First nor the Second World War originated from a direct confrontation between "great powers." The "great powers" were dragged into the First War as the result of a conflict between Austria-Hungary and Serbia and entered World War II in response to German aggression against Poland. By shielding the smaller powers through a common alliance, the greater powers provide for themselves an armour against hostile entanglements. As the material recipients of security, the smaller allies at the same time confer security benefits on their donors. This inverted logic, whereby donors are expected to be grateful to receivers for having the latter accept their gift of protection, recalls King Duncan's greeting of Lady Macbeth, when he asks her to be thankful for the labour he has caused her:

> Herein I teach you,
> How you shall bid God yield us for your pains,
> And thank us for your trouble.

Similarly, the greater powers are the co-recipients of the security benefits that are derived from the intra-Alliance adjustment and control process. A substantial share of the postwar reconciliation between former victims and aggressors, victors and vanquished, between Italy and Greece, between Germany and her western and Scandinavian neighbours, as well as the accommodation of disputes arising subsequently, may be attributed to the Alliance process of joint military planning and political adjustment. While the headlines have focused on the juxtaposition between common Alliance membership and the preservation of traditional resentments and antipathies, the gradual reconciliation has found direct expression in multilateral military arrangements. In 1960 Denmark agreed to provide the German army with supply bases in Jutland, and in December 1961, after considerable delay as the result of political opposition, COMBALTAP (Baltic Approaches Command) was created as part of NATO's North European Command for the purpose of keeping the seaway into the Baltic Sea open and to block enemy penetration into the North Sea. COMBALTAP involves German and Danish land, sea, and air forces as part of four sub-commands, one of which includes German and Danish naval units serving under a German admiral, and represents the first instance where a Scandinavian partner has agreed to serve under a German sub-regional commander. Roughly one third of the staff positions at COMBALTAP are held by Danish officers, the same proportion by German officers, with the remaining third being distributed among U.S., British, Norwegian, and Canadian officers.

Apart from their military qualification, this direct association of other allied officers also fulfills an important psychological role, for the Scandinavian powers had been reluctant to be drawn into a relationship of military intimacy with their stronger German neighbour unless this was accompanied by the mitigating presence of additional allied powers.

This particular concern reflects an instinctive predilection of the small powers in favour of regulating mutual security relations with their larger neighbours through a multilateral association rather than through a system of isolated bilateralism. The same instinctive reaction may be observed in the Canadian preference for retaining the option to conduct at least some of its military relations with its super-power neighbour through the multinational corridors of NATO rather than through direct channels.[2] Some of the opposition which was being voiced in Canada following the creation of NORAD in 1957 reflected this preference for multilateralism.

As the guardian of the American retaliatory force, NORAD was of considerable importance to the entire Alliance, although it was neither an integral part of NATO, nor responsible to that organization. The European allies, who did not doubt that the United States would defend itself against a direct attack, saw no reason to be associated in this North American continental defence effort which would involve extra costs without concrete benefits. This sentiment was clearly reflected by Secretary General Spaak's press conference in Ottawa in May 1958, which stressed that NORAD was neither a part nor an extension of NATO, nor under NATO command, and that NORAD matters were not being discussed by the Atlantic Alliance.[3]

Wishing to avoid public censure and to circumnavigate the delicate issue of parliamentary approval (for Parliament had not been asked to approve the agreement, though the government subsequently agreed to a general debate on NORAD), the Diefenbaker Government adopted the position that NORAD was an integral part of NATO.[4] While few Canadians questioned the practicality of an integrated

[2] Canadian professional military opinion does not necessarily share these reservations. In actual practice, NATO has very rarely been brought into play in order to help settle Canadian-U.S. defence relations. NORAD, overflight privileges, air base agreements, arrangements regarding radar and weather stations, and defence production agreements, have in fact all been concluded bilaterally without any need or desire on the part of the two contracting parties to involve NATO in this co-operative effort.

[3] *Montreal Star*, May 29, 1958.

[4] Canada, House of Commons, *Debates*, December 21, 1957, p. 2721.

North American air defence system at the time of its creation, the parliamentary debates on NORAD reveal both the
sensitivity of the issue in Canadian politics and the inherent
Canadian predilection for an approach which practises an
inverted form of Canning's dictum by calling into operation
the Old World through the multilateral association with
NATO in order to compensate for the imbalance of power in
the New World.[5]

A SMALLER ALLY'S PROBLEMS IN THE CHOICE
AND CONVERSION OF MILITARY ROLES

In Canada the original decision to station a Canadian air
division and an army brigade group in Europe had been
accepted without notable controversy. Politically and psy-
chologically this commitment has been rendered more tolerable to Canadian opinion by the fact that it constituted an
identifiable role under multilateral assignment which was
neither wholly defined nor directed by the United States.
The military importance of this contribution clearly did not
lie in its size but in the highly professional quality of personnel and the technically advanced level of equipment
which assisted SACEUR's task of raising the professional
level of the European forces. The military value of the
Canadian contingents in Europe has doubtlessly declined as
the result of the economic and military recovery of Europe.
Politically, however, a new premium has been placed on

[5] Mr. Pearson, as leader of the Liberal Opposition, denied that there
existed any direct link between NATO and NORAD, although he
wished that there were such union. Subsequently Mr. Pearson argued
that Canada should have used its assent to joining NORAD as a bargaining lever to get NORAD integrated into NATO and to reach in
equitable defence production agreement between Canada and the
United States. (*Debates*, March 2, 1959, p. 1498.) The strongest reservations to the bilateral nature of the NORAD agreement were voiced
in the ranks of the CCF party, which stressed that in surrendering her
sovereign rights to a bilateral rather than a multilateral organization,
Canada was placing herself in a position of political subordination
vis-à-vis the United States. (*Debates*, June 10, 1958, pp. 1020-21).

their presence in Europe, at least temporarily, as the result of recent developments in NATO. Their presence in Europe at this particular time serves to preserve the integrated system of defence in Europe against the disintegrative challenges posed by French action. It also helps protect the U.S. Congressional "flank" against pressure groups which advocate that the ever-widening orifice of Viet Nam be filled by means of a precipitate reduction of U.S. troops in Europe. The political importance of the Canadian forces in Europe stems from the fact that they underscore continental interdependence by actively involving both North American members in Europe and not only the United States.

In this manner the limited contribution of a smaller ally serves to underwrite the guarantee of a super-power. Its inherent value might best be measured in terms of the counterproductive effects that would result from a unilateral withdrawal. Recognition of this factor should in no way preclude the possibility of a future conversion of the role of the Canadian forces in Europe under less sensitive political circumstances. In part, this is already being realized by a growing commitment to the Allied Mobile Force, the AMF, whose task it is to protect NATO's remote northern and south-eastern flanks against minor conflicts or probing actions. It is a task that is particularly suited to smaller allies with a multi-purpose force and with a capacity for air mobility.

The AMF was set up following a recommendation by General Norstad in 1960. Its role is to provide a mobile allied defence in areas of potential tension and conflict on NATO's weakly defended flanks, such as northern Norway, northern Greece, and north-eastern Turkey. To some extent the Mobile Force is designed to extend to NATO's peripheral areas certain aspects of the integrated allied system of defence that already exists in the central sector of Europe. Apart from its strictly military utility, the AMF also serves the double political and strategic task of convincing both the adversary and the peripheral allies of the certainty that allied territory, regardless of its geographic location, would be defended collectively.

At present the AMF is composed of approximately 4 battalions each for the northern and south-eastern flank. Canada originally earmarked one battalion for AMF service and has now offered a second one.

For a smaller ally like Canada the prospect of making participation in the AMF the principal form of its direct contribution to the defence of Europe holds considerable attractions. The small size of the AMF, which is dictated both by military and political considerations, enables the smaller allies to play a relatively significant role in this Force.[6] Insofar as the Force is designed to help in the protection of the smaller allies and gives a prominent role to the smaller members, the AMF might be regarded as something of a small power league, combining several smaller powers for the protection of other allies of similar size.

For Canada there is the additional attraction that AMF requirements in terms of equipment, training, and transportation facilities are largely complementary to her peacekeeping role. In the event of an increased commitment to the AMF, this complementarity might be exploited by earmarking the same forces for a dual NATO flank and UN peacekeeping role. However, such amalgamation would require allied consensus on the utility of peacekeeping and the practicability of a dual interchangeable role.

But by converting her contribution to the defence of Europe solely to an active role in the AMF, Canada would raise some serious military and political questions. Whatever form the AMF will take, it will retain its relatively small size. The size principle of the Mobile Force is deter-

---

[6] Conceivably one might envisage a situation of tension and minor disturbances on the flanks when it would be useful to exclude the presence of U.S. contingents in order to reduce the risk of escalation. On the other hand, the absence of U.S. forces might be interpreted as lack of American support and would thus undermine the intended deterrent effect of the AMF.

mined by various strategic factors. In the first place, the remote geographic location and terrain of the flank areas would tend to make large-scale military operations extremely difficult. In the second place, it is unlikely that the adversary would willingly incur the risk of large-scale retaliation by directing major military thrusts against areas which are relatively inaccessible and, with developing missile technology, of low strategic value to him. Risks and possible gains would be so totally out of proportion that one could hardly credit a rational decision-maker with contemplating such a course of action. Thirdly, as in peacekeeping operations, the small size of the AMF contingents serves the purpose of providing a stabilizing "presence" while the introduction of major force units might act like a magnet in the sense of drawing increasingly larger forces to the particular trouble spot, instead of isolating the area of conflict. Consequently, there exists a rather narrow limit to the size of allied contributions to the AMF. Moreover, since the principal asset of the AMF lies in its collective nature, each member's scope for participation is even more severely restricted. Finally, it must be remembered that under the more favourable political climate in Europe and with the recent improvement of bilateral relations between the U.S.S.R. and Norway and Turkey respectively, the possibility that situations would arise which would require an Allied Mobile Force has declined markedly, and with it the emphasis on the Force.

If the Canadian military contribution to NATO were to be made solely through participation in the AMF, this would entail a very substantial reduction from the level of her previous commitments, both in terms of expenses, manpower, and equipment. A unilateral Canadian reduction of this kind would provide other allies with strong internal pressures and inducements to adopt a similar course of action. A smaller ally's reduction in commitments and military spending is much more likely to have a general effect on the Alliance and to set trends that would involve NATO at large than a unilateral policy of increased com-

mitments, which might solicit favourable mention at ministerial meetings but little in the line of concrete response
from other members.

These are issues which will have to be considered before
deciding on a conversion of military roles. On the other
hand, it must also be realized that a decrease in the size of
forces in the European area would constitute a progressive
and desirable outcome under more relaxed political conditions in Europe, provided such changes would proceed in
harmony with some accepted allied formula on defence
reductions and would coincide with, or generate, reciprocal
changes in the level of forces in Eastern Europe. If the latter
conditions are met, a smaller ally's military role conversion
might have a considerable impact on the political evolution
in Europe.

ALLIANCE MEMBERSHIP: POLITICAL GAINS AND INHIBITIONS

Alliance membership not only involves the participating
powers in military commitments and certain risks, but it
also imposes on them certain restraints which inhibit
their behaviour in the international political sphere. Just as
the United States was formerly persuaded to mute its anti-
colonial stand in UN debates lest it offend its NATO partners with colonial holdings, even at the risk of antagonizing
the newly emerging Afro-Asian nations, several NATO allies
now see fit to repress the impulse to criticize overtly U.S.
policy and objectives in Viet Nam, even at the expense of
incurring criticism at home and abroad. To the champions
of absolute national independence in foreign policy, these
self-imposed alliance inhibitions cause much mental an-
guish. However, alliance obligations, like marriage, generally seem to survive the inhibiting circumstances of the
contractual relationship.

It would seem that the temporary restraint on U.S. policy on the colonial issue, which kept the lines of communication open to both sides, enhanced its mediatory role to a

greater degree than open and vehement support for either side could have accomplished. In the long run, therefore, the policy of restraint, which was partly the result of U.S. membership in NATO, paid more substantive dividends to the principal American interest in an orderly decolonization process than the unrestrained exercise of its freedom of choice. Perhaps the same conclusion may eventually also be reached in the context of Viet Nam.

Participation in a common security framework is but one among several factors which cements the degree of interdependence among the industrialized powers of the Atlantic area. Interdependence neither removes separate national interests nor does it impose a ban on the expression of such interests. This is clearly borne out by the experience of conflicting opinions in the NATO Council and the low level of "bloc voting" by NATO members in the United Nations. However, once it is acknowledged that a high level of interdependence exists, it necessarily follows that separate national interests are most effectively realized not by a strategy that defends these interests in a vacuum of sovereign isolation but by one which seeks to influence the wider interdependent environment to which it feels bound by common interest and sentiment. Efforts to influence the wider framework from within, in this case through active membership in an alliance, impose restraints both on the style and content of a nation's foreign policy, especially in connection with intra-alliance relations and security questions. Non-aligned countries are not subject to the same kind of inhibitions. But much of their apparent independence is of the kind which is verbally assertive but factually ineffective, for it neither removes their dependence on the super-powers nor does it maximize their influence to the extent that could be achieved through a regular process of multilateral adjustment within an interdependent community.

There has always been a notable power discrepancy between the "great powers" and the smaller ones under the "balance of power" system. However, the present power discrepancy between the smaller members of NATO and the United States is without historical parallel. In addition, there has been a loss of flexibility insofar as the smaller allies can no longer opt for membership in shifting alliance coalitions with the same freedom as formerly. Despite this loss of manoeuvrability, the policies of the smaller allies now have a more significant bearing on the fate of the inter-dependent and interacting major powers than previously. In terms of their capacity to influence the behaviour of the greater powers, the smaller members of the Alliance may thus be able to report a net gain, all the more as they are now permanent co-actors in the multilateral political con-sultation process.

The process of consultation is one of primary means whereby smaller allies can individually or collectively exert an influence on policy decisions which affect the Alliance. The 1956 Report of the Committee of Three on Non-Mili-tary Co-operation in NATO, the so-called "Three Wise Men," defines consultation as follows:

> Consultation within an alliance means more than ex-change of information, though that is necessary. It means more than letting the NATO Council know about national decisions that have already been taken; or trying to enlist support for those decisions. It means the discus-sion of problems collectively, in the early stages of pol-icy formation, and before national positions become fixed. At best, this will result in collective decisions on matters of common interest affecting the Alliance. At the least, it will ensure that no action is taken by one mem-ber without a knowledge of the views of the others.[7]

Under the original Treaty terms of Article IV, provision for consultation was made only for circumstances when, in the opinion of an ally, its "territorial integrity, political inde-pendence or security" were threatened. But as it has evolved in NATO practice, consultation constitutes a continuous and regular process rather than an emergency measure. The practice of consultation has been supplemented by the

[7] Cited in NATO Information Service, *NATO: Facts About the North Atlantic Treaty Organization* (Utrecht: Bosch, 1962), p. 265.

guidelines which were provided by the 1956 Report and by the creation of the Committee of Political Advisers, acting under the authority of the Council and functioning under the chairmanship of the Assistant Secretary General for Political Affairs. In addition, the Oslo Conference of 1961 agreed on a measure to improve the confused state of consultation by forming temporary committees consisting of powers with a direct interest in a specific area, such as Africa or Asia, which would attempt to keep members aligned or more aware of policy differences in areas where Alliance partners were exposed to embarrassing conflicts.

Consultation constitutes nothing less than a voluntary self-denying ordinance on the unhindered exercise of national sovereignty in decision-making. It is an obligation that applies to all members alike and may be said to have been violated by all members on various occasions. Insofar as the decisions of the major NATO allies are more consequential and far-reaching in effect, the obligation to consult rests most heavily on the shoulders of the latter and the failure of observance among them is most heavily felt, so much so that one gains the entirely misleading impression which regards all shortcomings as the responsibility of the major powers.

Consultation is the means whereby the greater powers acknowledge their interdependence with the smaller allies. The smaller powers regard consultation as a matter of right rather than of courtesy in an alliance which is composed of sovereign states. This thinking underlay the recent warning by Norway's Under-Secretary of Foreign Affairs, Jens Boyesen, that if "the Alliance should cease to have day-to-day reality as a practical system of military and political cooperation, public opinion in many countries might become opposed to taking the risks that are necessarily involved in any allied partnership.[8]

It is therefore not surprising that the smaller powers

[8] Jens Boyesen, "Contributions of Small Powers to the Alliance", Cited in Edgar Furniss, Jr., *op. cit.*, p. 116.

have most actively supported the process whereby consultation has evolved in NATO practice. In 1952 a major structural reorganization of the Alliance was undertaken. This created the post of Secretary General and "streamlined" the North Atlantic Council so as to absorb the functions that had hitherto been conducted separately and more sporadically by the Committee of Foreign Ministers and their Council of Deputies, the Defence Committee, and the Defence Financial and Economic Committee. The plan of "streamlining" and centralizing the Alliance was first put forward by the Canadian government after the Korean War had emphasized the need for a swift rearmament of the West. The plan could hardly have succeeded at the very beginning of the Alliance. "Then", as a *New York Times* feature article pointed out, "all twelve powers were new to the game; the small powers mistrusted the big ones; civilians distrusted the military. Now we have worked side by side for eighteen months and we all see need for a single control and direction."[9]

Similarly, the principal charter for consultation, the 1956 Report of the "Three Wise Men", was drawn up by representatives of smaller or middle powers. Furthermore, the post of NATO Secretary General, the linchpin of the consultative process, has, with the exception of the first incumbent, been occupied by a national of one of the smaller powers.

The process of consultation comprises such diverse elements as the exchange of information; the submission of policy proposals before their enactment by individual allies for the purpose of general discussion and, tentatively at least, also adaptation in accordance with the views of the other allies; and policy-making, that is the collective formulation of allied aims and policies. The restricted nature of contacts, intelligence, and interests which smaller allies

[9] *New York Times*, March 18, 1952. For a further comment on Canada's role in improving NATO's infrastructure for consultation, see Lord Ismay, *NATO: The First Five Years* (Utrecht: Bosch, 1955), p. 41.

maintain in relation to more remote geographic regions imposes definite limits on their sources of information on many foreign policy issues. But accurate and full information must be regarded as a prerequisite for any meaningful participation in the formulation of Alliance policy and the exertion of influence on major allies. Without access to information, smaller allies would inevitably be reduced to a more passive foreign-policy role both within and outside the Alliance framework.

Regarding the policy functions of the Alliance, the smaller members, like constitutional monarchs, fulfil the role of supporting, restraining, warning, and encouraging the policies and proposals of their major partners. As George Liska observes, this role is partly political but largely representative, as it is concerned with preserving the smaller allies' status as sovereign states.

> Most lesser allies take a realistic view of their proper share in consultations. Their main concern is a formal one. They wish to be consulted in a way which would give a decent semblance of reality to their standing as partners and to the representative character of the major ally's diplomacy. Only when they are directly involved do lesser allies demand the right of veto as well as that of remonstrance.[10]

The above-cited paragraph may leave a somewhat exaggerated impression of the so-called veto powers of the smaller powers in NATO. Since NATO is an alliance of sovereign states and not a supranational institution, no specific allied defence programme or official NATO doctrine can be adopted without the unanimous agreement of its members. This rule of unanimity applies to such specific matters as the preparation of a communiqué following a ministerial meeting, agreement on NATO force levels, or acceptance of a formula for sharing the costs of NATO's infrastructure programme. But technically speaking, it is improper to talk of a veto. For in the first place, the veto act is linked to the

[10] George Liska, *Nations in Alliance: The Limits of Interdependence* (Baltimore: Johns Hopkins Press, 1962), p. 74.

process of voting, but neither the Council nor any other NATO organization reaches decisions by official or secret voting procedures. Secondly, when members consult on matters which do not specifically relate to NATO but involve their national foreign or defence policy, they are not legally restricted from implementing their original proposals, even if these should meet with some objections from among their allies. But in cases where consultation reveals differences, allies usually make an attempt to accommodate their policy in such a way as to make it more acceptable to the other NATO members. Even with respect to specific NATO projects, such as the creation of the nuclear planning group, lack of unanimity does not necessarily prevent the adoption of the majority proposal, if the dissenting member, in this particular case France, does not object to the other allies participating in a programme with which it refuses to be associated.

NATO is by no means the only forum where consultation between smaller and great powers takes place. Such consultation also takes place on a strictly bilateral basis, though here one might suppose that at least in some cases, let us say in consultation between the U.S. and Sweden, both the content and frequency of the process may have increased as the result of a spill-over from NATO consultations between the U.S. and Sweden's Scandinavian neighbours. In strictly quantitative terms, and in many instances also in terms of importance, the UN represents the principal forum for consultation between great and small powers.

Consultation in an alliance framework is no unmitigated blessing. Too rigid an adherence to the requirement to consult would not only heighten the dissatisfaction that would arise under those inevitable situations of improper consultation, but might also impair the military effectiveness of NATO by delaying or diluting necessary military measures. Advance consultation between the United States and its allies before the 1962 Cuban crisis would have impaired the premium which had to be placed on time and secrecy. In addition, the Cuban crisis presents a clear example of a situation where, despite subsequent allied criticism of not having been consulted, prior consultation would have placed the other allies before an agonizing choice of supporting the American proposal—and thus staking their survival on an issue that was not regarded as a primary security concern to themselves—or of opposing such a policy. Under the emergency conditions the negative reaction of its allies would hardly have restrained U.S. policy, but it would have imposed serious strains on NATO relations and might have provided a precedent for a similar U.S. refusal of assistance under conditions involving a primary European security need. Because of these circumstances many allies might privately have preferred to be exempted from this agonizing choice by being informed rather than consulted on U.S. intentions. Similarly, any rigid insistence on consultation under circumstances that clearly indicate that no agreement can be reached would tend to crystallize allied dissent and magnify frustrations. However, while this may be a sound generalization, it has the dangerous implication of justifying any failure to consult under the pretext or *a priori* assumption that agreement was impossible.

At first sight it seems that the difficulties of forming consensus would be multiplied by the admission of several smaller powers to the common consultative process. If anything, the contrary may be observed in actuality. In the first place, the Council does not as a general rule seek to establish a set of specific and definite decisions other than in discharging its routine financial and administrative duties. In the broader political and strategic field the Council is more concerned with establishing consensus on general principles and concepts, exploring the uncharted areas where common agreement may be possible, always trying to widen the boundaries of consent, while carefully circumnavigating the danger zones of recognized conflict issues. In this particular process, the smaller nations, which have a particular interest in maintaining agreement among the major members, have either used their special relations with one or more of the major allies or have tried to reach an understanding among themselves on specific issues in order to facilitate compromise among the major partners. "There is hardly any evidence", writes Under-Secretary Boyesen, an old NATO hand,

> that, when the initial positions of the major powers differ, they find it easier to reach agreement by themselves than in the presence of smaller allies. At the risk of generalizing a bit too much, I would say that the smaller countries have a tendency to seek for compromise when consultation might otherwise be ended.[11]

The smaller powers have carefully cultivated the art of assisting in political compromise schemes among the major powers. This finesse may, in part, be attributed to a flexibility in approach which is derived from sharing fewer international burdens and from manning the rear trenches of international conflict. It is also a self-defence mechanism whereby the smaller allies seek to preserve their separate identities by combatting the suffocating rigidity of doctrinal or extreme positions. Excessive conformity of Alliance thinking on all issues would threaten to destroy the separate identities of the smaller members, for it would make NATO policy synonymous with U.S. policy. Visions of a utopian future too often bear the mirrored image of current superpower policy. The insistence by the smaller members that NATO is an alliance this side of paradise may be discouraging to the idealist. It is not, however, without benefit in the practical management of the affairs of the Alliance.

The art of compromise, which the smaller allies have to some extent applied successfully in adjusting divergencies among the major allies, has also been applied in the direction of accommodating East-West relations. Even during the cold war freeze, the smaller allies strove to keep at least a narrow channel open for East-West communication.

At present the partial *détente* in East-West relations allows for direct communication and limited co-operation between the two super-powers which are linked through a

[11] Jens Boyesen, *op. cit.*, pp. 110-111.

community of parallel burdens. Under these circumstances the potential of the smaller allies to act as communications links between the super-powers has been reduced. Still, one can envisage conflict situations, as for example in Viet Nam, where the super-power dialogue suffers from a partial or regional paralysis. It is in situations of this kind that the creative diplomacy of the smaller allies, especially those who combine familiarity with the workings of the Alliance with expertise in specific regional conflict zones, could assist in maintaining a flexible system of East-West communications.

One can observe certain similar characteristics in concepts and behaviour which prevail among the smaller NATO powers. One of these is an instinctive antipathy to great-power triumvirates, whether conceived as a great-power directorate along the lines of the 1958 proposal by General de Gaulle, or as a special nuclear group of the nuclear "haves" and participants in a nuclear "hardware" solution. Even in cases, such as the contingency planning efforts during the Berlin crisis, where the need for a more restrictive form of consultation among NATO's major allies was recognized, the smaller members objected to being excluded from discussing more far-reaching but related questions, such as the preparation for a summit conference. Following a Canadian proposal, which was backed by the other smaller allies, it was therefore agreed that the special sessions of NATO's "Big Four" would coincide with the plenary meetings of the Foreign Ministers of the Atlantic powers so that there could be general consultation before and after the meetings of the Four.

Another general characteristic of the smaller allies has been their reluctance to expand the region of NATO commitments. This reluctance may be attributed in part to the more purely regional orientation of their concern and the fear of courting retaliation aginst their home territories as the result of foreign ventures. In part it also derives from unwillingness to spread their limited resources over too wide a radius. Considerable opposition was thus encountered from the ranks of the smaller powers to the original inclusion of Portugal and Iceland and subsequently to the admission of Greece and Turkey. This restrictive principle has created certain problems in the consultative process, for while it is generally accepted that the problems of peace are global and not regional and that no artificial geographic barriers can be imposed on consultation, several smaller powers have "felt that there must be some reasonable limitation upon the responsibilities and commitments which small countries can reasonably undertake as a consequence of NATO membership."[12] Another limitation on consultation has been the smaller allies' lack of intelligence or interest in regions other than the Atlantic area.

The smaller allies have thus been faced with the predicament of supporting the principle of extensive consultation in NATO in order to increase their influence in international affairs, while at the same time fearing that such consultation might form the first step toward an extended commitment. This dilemma was first encountered with the 1952 NATO Council resolution that gave moral support to the French position in Indo-China. The resolution was subsequently widely criticized in Denmark and Norway as implying an extension of national commitments in a manner that was unrealistic for a small European power. Norway's former Foreign Minister, Halvard Lange, placed his finger on the nerve of the problem when he wrote that

> for a small country, in particular, political consultation cuts both ways. It is temptingly convenient to stay aloof and criticize decisions taken by other countries after they have been made and in the light of subsequent events. It is a different matter to have the opportunity to state in advance the point of view of your country and to take your share of the responsibility. As far as Norway is concerned we have accepted the fact that with added opportunities for influencing policy goes added responsibility for the decisions taken.[13]

[12] Jens Boyesen, *op. cit.*, p. 112.
[13] Halvard Lange, "NATO Needs the Capacity to Anticipate," *Globe and Mail*, April 26, 1954.

While Canada has been similarly unwilling to accept a regional extension of her commitments under NATO, she has generally been in favour of maximizing both the range of topics and the geographic area covered by the consultative process. Perhaps this might be explained by the fact that Canada, because of her broader bicontinental military commitments, has tended to show more sensitivity to the interdependence of international issues than the smaller European allies with a purely regional commitment and orientation. Furthermore, Canada forms an integrated strategic unit with the United States and can thus not entertain any reasonable hope of escaping from a general escalation that may arise from U.S. involvements outside the Atlantic region.

A similar tendency to give a more extensive interpretation to NATO functions than is generally encountered among the smaller members of the Alliance can be witnessed in the popular Canadian sentiment in favour of giving literal application to Article II of the Treaty. This article, which was originally inserted in response to Canada's initiative and insistence, aimed at achieving two basic policy goals. In the first place, Article II reflected the belief that European stability depended on economic as well as on military factors and that NATO's protective security barricades would stimulate Europe's political, economic and spiritual recovery. The idea of a liberalized and co-operative pattern of economic relations along transatlantic channels was in harmony with the Canadian concern for offsetting her increasing economic dependence on the United States, as this could no longer be achieved by reliance on British and Commonwealth ties. From a Canadian point of view, therefore, the political and economic inclusion of continental Europe in a common NATO framework promised to restore a degree of North American continental balance which had been destroyed by the partial erosion of the British counterweight.

In the second place, the idealistic tenor of Article II served the cause of political expediency in reconciling Canadian public opinion in general, and the CCF in particular, to the unprecedented step of entangling the country in a peacetime alliance.

Article II has subsequently become a political bestseller on the Canadian domestic scene, so much so that its spiritual inventors have been somewhat embarrassed by repeated public demands to give concrete institutional form to this statement of principle,[14] and have been forced to insert a muting note of sober realism. As early as 1952, the Canadian Ambassador, Mr. Arnold Heeney, advised caution in relation to the actual execution of Article II.

> I am going to suggest . . . that we shall make our best progress toward the objectives stated in Article II if we are willing to look beyond the North Atlantic Organization for areas and opportunities of non-military collaboration. There is nothing in our Treaty to suggest that NATO is the only means by which we are to build our community.[15]

[14] Canadian Members of Parliament have on numerous occasions requested that Article II be invoked for such concrete issues as compelling the United States to adopt a lower level of tariffs or to discontinue its international wheat dumping practices. See, for example, Canada, House of Commons, *Debates*, December 11, 1953, pp. 824-825.

[15] Arnold Heeney, Address delivered at Oxford University to the Atlantic Community Conference, September 10, 1952. Cited in Canada, Department of External Affairs, *Statements and Speeches 1952*, No. 37, p. 3. The same sentiment was reflected in Mr. Dana Wilgress' speech to the Vancouver Board of Trade on May 20, 1953, which portrayed Article II as "a watching brief over these [non-military] forms of activity rather than an opportunity for executive action. It is the task of NATO to see that its members follow harmonious policies in these fields. The implementation of these policies can best be left to action through the medium of the 'Specialized Agencies'." (Canada Department of External Affairs, *Statements and Speeches 1953*, No. 24, p. 6.)

Speaking in the same vein, External Affairs Secretary Paul Martin stated more recently that it "was never the intention to transform the North Atlantic Treaty Organization from a military into an economic alliance. . . . Much of what was intended by Article II—I do not say all—is now being done by OECD and under GATT, particularly following the initiative of the late President of the United States." (Canada, House of Commons, *Debates*, April 1, 1964, p. 1673)

In conclusion it should be emphasized that despite their diminishing role in terms of a strictly military contribution, the smaller NATO allies have become firmly established in the communal political functions of the Alliance. In this sphere they have left an impressive record of offering initiative and compromise solutions. The very limitation of their military role may in fact account for the smaller members' tendency to seek to improve and augment the political functions of NATO. The role of the smaller allies has not been that of ineffective backbenchers.

6
Alliances in the Nuclear Age

WHEN SEEN FROM an historical perspective, alliances appear so frequently in association with highly competitive or conflict situations that they seem to represent an almost permanent feature in the conduct of international relations. Despite this permanence in the existence of alliances, their functions have undergone considerable transformation as the result of changes in the international system. NATO, a product of the cold war and a bipolar international environment, operated in a very different manner from alliances during the classical "balance of power" system, and, given the waning of the former bipolar system, it is no longer the same alliance that it originally was. In order to gain a better basis from which to explain and predict future changes in the role of the North Atlantic Alliance, it will be necessary to examine the recent transformation in the international environment.

Various attempts have been made to analyze the principal characteristics of the present system. This has proved to be a particularly arduous task, for not only does the present system lack historical precedents but it also provides us with inadequate data because of its very recent origin and embryonic stage of development. The task of definition and explanation is made even more complicated by the fact that the present system combines elements of bipolarity, while no longer being purely bipolar, with those of multipolarity, without having become fully polycentric or necessarily proceeding in the direction of unrestricted multipolarity.

George Liska characterizes the present international system as "quasi-multipolar in behavior and mixed bipolar-multipolar in the structure of capabilities", and concludes that the "pattern of behavior predominates over the pattern of capabilities whenever a balance neutralizes conflicting capabilities on one or the other level."[3]

Another commentator talks in terms of "partially neutralized bipolarism".[4] Wolfram Hanrieder uses the label "hetero-symmetrical bipolarity".[5] R. N. Rosecrance speaks of "bi-multipolarity".[6] This writer has referred to a "three-tiered multidimensional system within a bipolar setting."[7] What all of these labels have in common, other than a somewhat forbidding hyphenated nomenclature, is the concept of duality in a system which simultaneously embraces some characteristics of the bipolar and multibloc systems.

When the term polycentrism was first coined by Togliatti in an interview with the paper *Nuovi Argomenti* in June 1956, it referred to the increasing number of options that were becoming available to national Communist parties, to non-aligned countries, and even to committed allies in

[3] George Liska, *op. cit.*, p. 162.
[4] Wilhelm Cornides, "German Unification and the Power Balance", *Survey*, No. 58 (January 1966), p. 142.
[5] Wolfram Hanrieder, "The International system: bipolar or multibloc?", *Journal of Conflict Resolution*, IX, No. 3 (September 1965), p. 306.
[6] R.N. Rosecrance, "Bipolarity, multipolarity, and the future", *Journal of Conflict Resolution*, X, No. 3 (September 1966), p. 322.
[7] Harald von Riekhoff, "The Atlantic Alliance and the Strategic Equilibrium", in Adam Bromke & Philip Uren, eds., *The Communist States and the West* (New York: Praeger, 1967), pp. 54-78.

choosing centres of political and ideological guidance, cultural contacts, and economic assistance. While polycentrism correctly denotes a proliferation in the volume of inter-state contacts and an increase in the range of political options, it should not be treated as representing the equalization of military and economic strengths of the super-powers and the capabilities of nations from other categories of power. Despite the emergence of quasi-independent centres of nuclear decision-making, the inequality in terms of military power which exists between the super-power category and others has increased, is increasing, and shows few signs of diminishing. What has emerged in the shadow of the relative security under the super-power nuclear equilibrium are new sources of guidance and inspiration and "new centres of ambition",[8] not new centres of miltary power.

In relation to nuclear weapons, the system has lost none of its bipolar attributes. The emergence of independent nuclear "trigger" powers has not significantly altered this state of nuclear bipolarity. Only the development of a fully effective nuclear second-strike force approximating that of the U.S. and U.S.S.R. could cause the system to move to one of nuclear multipolarity. But with respect to economic capabilities the international system has lost many of its bipolar aspects, especially after the emergence of regional economic groupings. Multipolarity exerts itself most noticeably with respect to political behaviour, political and cultural leadership, aspirations and ambitions.

In major security questions and acute crisis situations over issues such as Berlin or Cuba, the bipolar element still tends to dominate the international system. Within these increasingly less restrictive limits, however, multipolarity characterizes international behaviour in routine political relations and economic transactions. Nuclear bipolarity imposes certain limits to the free unfolding of multipolar or polycentric behaviour, but at the same time it acts as a

[8] Theo Sommer, "For an Atlantic Future", *Foreign Affairs*, Vol. 43 No. 1 (October 1964), p. 113.

source for polycentrism. For it is precisely the strategic equilibrium of nuclear weapons which inhibits the super-powers' freedom of action and thereby enhances the political manoeuvrability of the other allies. Henry Kissinger correctly summarizes the situation when he observes that "polycentrism is on the rise not because the world has ceased to be bipolar, but because with respect to nuclear weapons it essentially remains so."[9]

SUPER-POWER RELATIONS UNDER A SYSTEM OF BI-MULTIPOLARITY

The present tendency toward pluralism in political behaviour within a system which, in terms of physical power, is still largely characterized by bipolarity, is due less to a breakthrough on the political or ideological level than to the emergence of a stable equilibrium of nuclear deterrence. The profound changes that have taken place in relations between the super-powers and in the behaviour within and between the two major alliances must largely be attributed to this development in weapons technology. The transformation has brought havoc into traditional alliance concepts and has created a bizarre situation where the chief protagonists rely on mutual co-operation, and "where neutrals enjoy most of the protection of allies and allies aspire to have the same freedom of action as neutrals."[10]

But given this strategic basis, the principal political developments which are derived from it acquire their own self-generating momentum and logic. Under the present system of bi-multipolarity, relations between the two super-powers involve a mixed element of conflict and co-operation. At best, these relations may be characterized as a *détente* but not as an *entente*. And unless China emerges as a direct challenger of super-power dimensions, it would be unrealistic to expect the two existing powers—Peking's accusations notwithstanding—to form a mutual alliance against

[9] Henry Kissinger, *op. cit.*, p. 17.
[10] *Ibid.*, p. 18.

China or any other power or inferior coalition of powers. The principal areas of conflict which marked the cold war period remain: ideological cleavages; a deadlock of over two decades standing over a European settlement; and the failure to reach a comprehensive arms control or disarmament agreement. To these come more recent issues such as the war in Viet Nam. But in all of these cases the pitch of conflict has been lowered and the style of confrontation has been altered, as both sides recognize growing areas of complementary interests beside the elements of discord. Both protagonists share a common interest in avoiding mutual annihilation; third-source conflict situations which are removed from super-power initiative and influence yet involve the risk of escalation; and reckless arms race that would be militarily provocative and economically destructive. But this alignment against undesired, uncontrollable and risky eventualities is not a super-power alliance against other powers, even though the mutual concern of Moscow and Washington in containing Chinese expansion bears some resemblance to a common policy of containment.

THE ROLE OF ALLIANCES IN A BI-MULTIPOLAR SYSTEM

The present system of alliances has its origin in the preceding bipolar system. In the meantime, at least a partial systems change has occurred. It is therefore necessary to examine how the existing alliances, especially NATO, are adapting to the changed international conditions or whether they rigidly adhere to previous models of behaviour. If the latter were true, an alliance such as NATO would represent not merely an anachronism but also an impediment to a further modification of the international system in a direction which, by general accord, is regarded as preferable to an unmodified bipolar system.

Under the "balance of power" system alliances usually served the purpose of assisting in the actual conduct of war. In addition alliances served the function of conferring status on their members. The desire to confer status on a particular power was of special significance in cases where geographically remote powers were brought into the central European system. In part at least, the Anglo-Japanese alliance of 1902 was designed to serve this particular purpose. A more frequent use of the status-rendering functions of alliances was made in those cases where previously minor actors sought recognition as "great powers" and membership in the European Concert. It was this motive, and not any direct strategic interests which Sardinia had in that conflict, which prompted Cavour's unusual decision to join in the remote Crimean War on the side of Britain and France. In that particular situation both the established "great powers" and the "status seekers" found in the alliance a useful mechanism for realizing their political goals. The latter gained in status, and the former were able to assist in the emergence of a new power and prospective partner for future coalitions.

The third major function of alliances under the "balance of power" system was that of promoting international stability through intra-alliance control. Statesmen like Bismarck utilized the system of intra-alliance control with consummate skill and great finesse. One of the principal advantages to Germany of the *Drei Kaiserbund* lay in the fact that it offered German diplomacy the opportunity to mediate and adjust conflict situations between her two allies, Russia and Austria-Hungary. Similarly, from the German point of view, the chief importance of Italy as a member of the Triple Alliance lay less in the latter's possible military contribution in the event of war—there was little illusion in Berlin about Italian military effectiveness—than in providing Germany with a lever to prevent the outbreak of war between Austria and Italy. German diplomacy under Bismark feared a general European conflagration and availed itself of this kind of peacekeeping mechanism which tied the arms of the prospective adversaries through the preventive bonds of tripartite alliances.

The primary purpose of alliances under the period of

bipolarity was not so much to improvise a collective defence effort after war had broken out but to improve the preparation for war in order to deter the outbreak of military conflict.

The element of deterrence was not altogether lacking under the "balance of power" system, but it was much less important and operated in a different manner, as it relied on a pre-conflict advertisement of the expected coalition array and thus tried to persuade an adversary that his goals would be denied. Under nuclear bipolarity the element of denial plays a less important role in the deterrent function than the threat of massive retaliation, where costs would be out of all proportion to any gain which an aggressor could possibly expect.

The preoccupation of alliances under the bipolar period was with maintaining military stability through a balance of terror, rather than with seeking political stability through intra-alliance and inter-alliance accommodation and negotiation.

The shift to the present mixed bi-multipolar system has brought with it major changes in the function of alliances. One effect of this change has been the notable downgrading of the status-conferring functions of alliances. In an international situation which is marked by greater flexibility and which places a new premium on national independence, non-alignment rather than alliance membership is regarded as a status symbol. Some allies are consequently seeking to remove the inhibiting effects of alliance membership, as they are vying with non-aligned powers in the assertion of their regained or newly won independence. Those nations which now seek to win international recognition of their independence or want to upgrade their accepted status in the international community try to achieve this aim through UN membership rather than adherence to an alliance with a super-power. In other cases, powers might seek to augment their independent status by developing a national nuclear force, if this option is available to them.

Insofar as the present system is a mixed one which still retains the characteristics of bipolarity with respect to military capabilities, it seems natural that the need to provide for a deterrence posture should, as was true during the preceding bipolar system, still remain the most important immediate rationale of NATO's continued existence. This need is recognized by all allies, including France.

There would be a declining need for an allied deterrent system if the imbalance of military forces in the European area were to be adjusted and if co-operation between the two super-powers were to continue and to expand.

So far the bi-multipolar system has been characterized by considerable changes in the general political atmosphere of East-West relations and by an expanding volume of contacts and transactions. But these changes in economic behaviour and political style have not yet met with any reciprocal measures in the form of reducing the concentration and imbalanced distribution of military forces in the European area. What has changed is not the destructive power of the military forces of the Soviet Union and its Eastern European allies, which in physical terms is greater than ever, but the general political climate in which these forces operate.

Before this general easing of tensions in the political and economic sphere will also be matched by concrete accommodation measures in the military field, it is unlikely that the West European allies would be willing to dispense entirely with the reinsurance which they gain through membership in the Alliance.

NATO AND INTERNATIONAL STABILITY

Under the bipolar system the role of alliances was to preserve international stability by enforcing a precarious nuclear truce, while the political situation in Europe remained essentially frozen. Given the more flexible and mobile conditions of today's international system, multilateral alliances such as NATO might become increasingly important as a stabilizing mechanism under conditions of rapid political change. What is desired in the European situation is a political transformation that would overcome the present division without military conflict or the imminent threat of such conflict, and without the violent overthrow of the existing political and social order.

The dual task of promoting political change and political stabilization need not necessarily be complementary in nature. One approach to political stabilization, especially if pursued by a military alliance, might be a policy of rigid adherence to the *status quo*, as the result of a natural aversion to all new and not fully predictable experiments. To some extent NATO has manifested this orientation. Its role in maintaining the territorial *status quo* in Europe against acts of aggression may lead to a preference for the political *status quo* as well. But at the same time the second most important aim of the Alliance is to create favourable conditions for a settlement of Europe's political problems. This original aim is reinforced by the allied pledge to support the cause of German reunification, which has thus become a moral commitment for the Alliance, as well as a real political burden, for under a more vigorous German assertion on behalf of reunification, which one will have to anticipate in the near future, the case cannot be expected to remain dormant forever. In addition, the existence of NATO has been more consequential in promoting those forces which have generated political change in Europe than has been reflected in official NATO policy and ministerial communiqués. A growing feeling of security is the prerequisite to the European allies' renewed political manoeuvrability and initiative in favour of a growing *détente* in Europe. At the present stage, this security is still very largely the result of the super-power nuclear stalemate extended to the European allies through the "deterrent-exporting" mechanism of a common alliance framework.

Under the political and strategic conditions existing today it is essential that the fundamental security needs of the European powers, the United States, and the Soviet

Union are not injured in the process of reaching a European settlement. To proceed otherwise would cause a massive reaction against this process of change and would thus foster a return to the rigidity of the preceding period of bipolarity. It might, furthermore, generate some desperate conflict-promoting responses by the exposed power.

The process of political settlement would require agreement on military measures which might involve certain risks and would certainly represent less than the optimum military posture. As George Kennan warns,

> the ideal military posture is simply the enemy of every political *détente* or compromise; and whoever is not prepared to make sacrifices and to accept risks in the military field should not lay claim to any serious desire to see world problems settled by any means short of war.[11]

By providing its members with a minimum security shield, NATO encourages them to accept and seek certain military and political innovations and experiments, even though these might involve some risk. In this manner the Alliance may be said to promote political change at least indirectly. At the same time the existence of the Alliance helps deter actions by individual members, or it acts as a shock absorber to actions which would have a destabilizing effect on the political situation in Europe. This is nowhere more evident than with reference to Germany, where the feeling of insecurity is higher than in any other West European power. NATO originally facilitated Germany's rearmament at a scale and in a form which constituted no security threat to her West European neighbours. The security benefits which Germany derives from the continued existence of the Alliance now enable her to refrain from unfolding her full military, including nuclear, potential, which she might otherwise feel compelled to do at the cost of renewed instability in Europe.

By accommodating German security needs, NATO shields the East European powers against the threat of a

<hr>

[11] George Kennan, "Disengagement Revisited", *Foreign Affairs*, Vol. 37, No. 2 (January 1959), p. 199.

renewed military expansion by Germany. Furthermore, the existence of NATO blunts the effectiveness of Soviet threats and pressures against Western Europe and therby enhances the manoeuvrability of the East European powers, for the ability of the West European powers to resist Soviet threats and pressures is one condition for greater East European independence from the Soviet Union. Similarly, the Warsaw Pact, even though it places the East European countries in a position of dependence on Moscow, provides them with the necessary security framework which in the net effect generates rather than represses East European tendencies of independent behaviour and the expression of distinct and separate national interests.

NATO'S INTERNAL STABILIZATION MECHANISM

The complexity, volume, and ramification of contacts and transactions among the powers of the North Atlantic area, with their high level of industrialization and standard of living, as well as technological sophistication, is not duplicated by any other area. The volume of transactions can no longer be accommodated by strictly improvised and bilateral means and must be supplemented by more permanent and multilateral practices and institutions. In this respect, NATO, through its continuous exchange of information and consultation, acts as a clearing-house at the highest political level. Even if the military rationale of the Alliance should cease, the need for a permanent central apparatus which could help accommodate these diverse political needs of a highly interdependent group of nations would remain. Such an organization might reappear under a different name, let us say, Atlantic Consultative Council; however, its functions would largely reflect the political work of the North Atlantic Treaty Organization at present. The existence of an organization of this nature represents a concession to the needs of interdependence.

In addition to its function as a political clearing-house among a group of intimately interrelated powers, NATO has also fulfilled the important role of facilitating the evolution toward a "security community" in the North Atlantic area. A "security community," as already defined in Chapter 3, refers to the emergence of practices and institutions which allow for the peaceful settlement of disputes among the participating countries. Not only the perception of an external threat, but also the process of organizing for a common defence in response to this threat, has had the indirect effect of yielding internal community benefits. The practice of joint planning and consultation enhances the propensity for political compromise and accommodation and increases the predictability of allied behaviour. Continuous exchange of information improves awareness of each other's policies and needs. Military and economic assistance furthers the process of mutual responsiveness.

Even if there has been some gradual gravitation toward a "security community" which embraces the entire North Atlantic area, and if one accepts the existence of regional "security communities", as between Canada and the United States, or Denmark and Norway, and perhaps also among the EEC partners, the existence of a plenary "security community" which includes the entire Atlantic region cannot yet be fully taken for granted. The British-Icelandic fisheries dispute, despite its *opera buffa* overtones, and the Cyprus conflict have painfully brought this to light. Both cases involved a temporary breakdown of the process of peaceful accommodation and involved the threat of force. Despite these setbacks, it is important to give NATO its due for having contributed to a pacific solution in one case, and to the avoidance of an open military conflict in the other.

An important role in mediating among NATO members and in strengthening the Atlantic "security community" is vested in the office of the Secretary General because of his prestige and right of initiative, "which gives to his position a certain amount of supranational character."[12] As de-

---

[12] Dirk Stikker, *op. cit.*, p. 7.

scribed by Mr. Stikker, a former incumbent of the office, the internal mediation functions of the Secretary General include the right to bring to the attention of the Council all matters threatening the solidarity and effectiveness of the Alliance, the right to correspond with governments, and the right to "offer his good offices to member governments in dispute, initiating—if his offer is accepted—procedures of inquiry, mediation, conciliation, or arbitration."[13]

NATO AND THE EVOLUTION OF EAST-WEST RELATIONS

Perhaps even more important than NATO's internal stabilization function in a period of political transformation is its stabilization role as it applies to changes in East-West relations.

The security which the super-powers derive from the nuclear equilibrium that now exists between them automatically also affects their European allies and provides them with greater freedom for independent action. Rather than trying to suppress these centrifugal trends, the super-powers should seek to stabilize this process within the existing, though changing, Alliance framework. The North Atlantic Alliance and the Warsaw Pact have the advantage of each combining within one organization one super-power with its respective sphere of maximum involvement in Europe. The alliance system thus serves to accommodate and regulate the *de facto* "presence" of the two super-powers in Europe. Even George Kennan, one of the spiritual fathers of the Western concept of disengagement, warns against the destabilizing effects which would result from a precipitate dissolution of the two parallel two-tiered alliance systems:

> And if the bonds of alliance and obligations to the two semi-European super-powers were to be severed, and the restraints implicit in those bonds suddenly to be removed, who is to say that the border problems, uncertainties, apprehensions, and manoeuvring for position

[13] *Ibid.*, pp.7-8.

which characterized the life of central and east Europe between the wars, would not reappear?[14]

Changes in the relations between the European partners of NATO and the East European members of the Warsaw Pact have complemented the altered nature of super-power relations. The resumption of contacts between the East European states and their Western counterparts has proceeded strictly along bilateral lines. Britain's effort to retain some degree of flexibility in diplomatic contacts and trade policy *vis-à-vis* Eastern Europe, which even continued during the cold war era, has now found a vivid echo in Gaullist policy of political and cultural advances to Eastern Europe. In a partial outflanking of the self-imposed restrictions of its Hallstein Doctrine, i.e., the refusal to maintain diplomatic relations with countries which recognize East Germany, the Federal Republic of Germany has embarked on a policy of economic engagement in Eastern Europe, which has been supplemented politically by the establishment of diplomatic relations with Rumania.

Accompanying the increase in bilateral relations between the East European and West European powers, there has been a marked growth in contacts between Western Europe and the Soviet Union, which finds its principal expression in General de Gaulle's present overtures toward Moscow. Despite the policy of "building bridges" toward Eastern Europe, which President Johnson announced in 1964 and more lately in October, 1966, developments in the relations between Washington and the East European capitals have so far failed to match the level of inter-Europe contacts. In part this may be attributed to the negative impact of the Vietnamese conflict; partly it can be explained by the fact that the East European countries still do not enjoy the same degree of freedom of initiative as their Western counterparts. Also the history of American involvement in Eastern Europe is in no way comparable to the close links which have

[14] George Kennan, "Europe in East-West Relations", *Survey*, No. 58 (January 1966), p. 122.

traditionally tied Russia with the West European powers as co-partners in the previous "balance of power" system.

In the initial phase of the delicate task of rebuilding contacts between Eastern and Western Europe, the more modest form of bilateralism may have produced better results than a collective NATO approach that might have stalled, either because of lack of agreement among NATO members or because of a Soviet reaction to this concerted approach, which might have taken the form of tighter control over Eastern Europe.

Despite the necessity of continuing these bilateral contacts as part of the strategy of active engagement in Eastern Europe, the exclusive reliance on the process of parallel and sometimes competitive bilateralism would be self-defeating and detrimental to the political goals of active engagement, the purpose of which is to involve both Western and Eastern Europe in a common multilateral framework. If the complex process of political engagement is to be brought to a fruitful synthesis without incurring the risks of counterproductive results in the form of allied suspicion, unnecessary duplication of programmes, and mutually destructive competition, it remains imperative that there be active consultation, exchange of information, and co-ordination of policy within a joint framework, as is presently provided by NATO.

At the moment those activities which are concerned with promoting relations between Eastern and Western Europe are largely confined to the sphere of increasing the volume of transactions, of broadening the range of human contacts, and of improving the general atmosphere. It would therefore be highly premature to speculate on the nature of formal negotiations that might eventually be held on the question of a European settlement. If an Atlantic alliance should still be in existence at that time, it might provide a useful forum in which a common allied platform could be drawn up prior to embarking on formal East-West negotiations. This would be all the more useful since it is unlikely that the majority of allies, though vitally concerned, would be given the opportunity to act as direct participants at such a conference, except perhaps during the final phase of negotiations, and as signatories to the final agreement.

Despite this potential alliance capacity, it would be unreasonable to expect NATO to become the clearing-house for all East-West activities. In the economic sphere, organizations such as GATT and UN Economic Commission for Europe, both including NATO and Warsaw Pact members, OECD, or the more constricted EEC forum, have important roles to play in the patient process of reassembling the pieces of a fragmented Europe. The North Atlantic Council is not a special agency for economic collaboration or cultural and intellectual co-operation; nor can it act as a forum whose exclusive preoccupation lies in the field of arms control planning. But it has the merit of being partly associated with all of these activities. By combining the assets of intimacy and informality with those of multisectoral involvement, the Council is admirably suited to function as a permanent caucus for the general accommodation of these interacting factors. Through the information and clearing-house functions of the NATO Council, allies can keep each other informed about their activities in various specialized agencies and the progress in their respective bilateral policies *vis-à-vis* Eastern Europe. Before addressing any major proposal to a wider forum, such as proposing a formula for German reunification to the Warsaw Pact, or presenting the Eighteen Nations Disarmament Conference with a European arms control blueprint, it would be useful to submit the embryonic proposal to the critical examination of the more restricted and homogeneous NATO caucus. One would thereby seek to accommodate different allied needs and gain a trial run for testing the wider acceptability of the plan, for if consensus could not be established among NATO members, the proposal is unlikely to solicit a more favourable reception in a wider forum.

It is neither possible nor desirable to impose on all NATO allies uniform standards of conduct in their relations with the East European states. But apart from the need to agree on some basic ground rules and to establish a mechanism for the co-ordination of these parallel efforts, a more far-reaching multilateral approach would be required if a major breakthrough is to be achieved in the political stalemate in Europe. "The day is over", writes Professor Brzezinski, "when purely bilateral economic ties with the Communist states constituted a net political gain for the West."[15]

No single issue shows the overlapping symmetrical features between the need for change and the necessity to preserve political stablility as strongly as the question of German reunification. The division of Germany is symptomatic of the present division of Europe and demonstrates this division in its crassest, most brutal, and most tangible form. One cannot proceed to rebuild a reunited Germany on the foundation of a divided Europe, just as an East-West *rapprochement* in Europe cannot be fully consummated without some form of German reunification. The existence of two Germanies is thus both symptom and cause for the perpetuation of the two Europes, and the elimination of both will have to proceed concurrently.

The new German coalition government has accepted the fact that reunification can be reached only by the gradual route of a *rapprochement* with Eastern Europe rather than by the previously held tactical approach of "negotiating from strength". Despite its euphemistic terminology, the policy of "negotiating from strength" in its final analysis evoked the image of Germany's historical experience of unification through *Blut und Eisen* or, in the present context, by the exploitation of the West's superiority in nuclear weapons in a policy of calculated pressures and threats.

The promissory note of allied support for the cause of reunification which Germany received in return for her entry into NATO may have contributed to her passive and reluctant attitude towards the policy of *détente* in Europe The allied promise seemed to shift the burden of under-

[15] Z. K. Brzezinski, "American Globalism", *Survey*, No. 58 (January 1966), p. 28.

taking concrete steps for Germany's reunification largely onto the shoulders of the other NATO powers and thus gave the German government a kind of alibi for entrenching itself behind the barricades of a rigid doctrinal stand. But more recently Germany seems to have adopted the example of her allies by cultivating bilateral dealings with the East European powers without insisting that irrevocable steps toward German reunification precede these contacts. Under Foreign Minister Schröder this took the form of a German economic engagement in Eastern Europe. The present government coalition in Germany has expanded this into the political sphere by renouncing the validity of the Munich Agreement of 1938 and by establishing diplomatic relations with Rumania. Recognition of the other East European governments except the D.D.R., might follow from this precedent.

German policy at present seems generally agreed that reunification cannot be achieved quickly by some acrobatic legal formula which would be arranged by a summit conference. Instead, reunification would follow as the result of a gradual evolution in the entire fabric of European economic and political life. Since this is a process of evolution it is a case where time will walk on crutches. Secondly, Bonn seems to have accepted that reunification will in part have to proceed by the collective road of a multilateral all-European solution, primarily in the economic field, in close association with the two super-powers. Despite this collective approach, reunification will, to some extent, have to be a do-it-yourself kit, relying on Germany's own initiative, programmes, and sacrifices. One fundamental sacrifice would be Germany's recognition of the Oder-Neisse line. This act would greatly restore German manoeuvrability and influence in Eastern Europe and provide a greater degree of counterpoise to the Soviet "presence" in that area than has existed since World War II. But the recognition of the Oder-Neisse line presents an immense political and emotional issue which Germany will have to resolve by herself, and it is hard to see how NATO could play a constructive role in this matter without incurring the risk of alienating Germany.

On the issue of an all-European association for economic co-operation, it should be noted that such a multilateral organization constitutes the best system for safely absorbing a reunited Germany into a joint European commonwealth without endangering the security of the East European partners.

One precondition for such an association might be the partial integration of Eastern Europe somewhat on the pattern of the European Six. This integrated posture would enable the East European powers to establish a relation of confidence *vis-à-vis* Germany and to gain sufficient independence to exist between the Soviet Union and an economically integrated Western Europe without fear of domination by either. Similarly, if the East European countries were to be economically integrated among themselves, they should find it safer to be intimately associated with a more dynamic and ideologically different Western Europe.

The obstacles to economic integration in Eastern Europe, as seen by the present COMECON experience, are enormous. These difficulties might even be magnified by the exclusion of the Soviet Union, for in such a case the Kremlin would reverse its present activity from a pro- to an anti-integration position. But without the restraining impact of Soviet influence or of an integrated economic community in that region, the countries of that area might demonstrate a growing tendency to revert to the open economic, and possibly also political, competition and conflict that characterized their relationship in the inter-war period, with its tariff warfare, border disputes, and quarrels about minorities.

In addition, it must be realized that the process of economic integration in Eastern Europe will encounter stronger inherent liabilities than those which originally confronted the West European Six. In the latter case the process of integration was facilitated by a mutual interplay between a flexible and decentralized system of free market economies, on the one hand, and some form of government direction, involvement, and partnership, on the other. But in the case of Eastern Europe, integration would have to cope with a more rigid pattern of monolithic government-controlled national economies.

While the West European political system can only have very little attraction for the East European political elites, the latter have not been immune to the magnetic appeal of the concrete economic results that have been achieved under the Common Market. The EEC, by the mere example of its existence as well as through direct assistance, could be of great importance in promoting a closer economic integration in Eastern Europe. Given this situation, it would seem that a multilateral economic approach towards Eastern Europe constitutes the West's most significant opportunity to instigate a fundamentally peaceful breakthrough that would take Europe out of its present stalemate and launch it onto the route of political settlement. This economic approach has the further benefit of being able to utilize an existing economic system and structure, without first having to wait for the unlikely, or at least very remote, emergence of an integrated West European political community.

By the process of economic engagement the East European powers should be brought into a permanent multilateral association with the European Common Market. The process might be facilitated if in the initial stage the East European powers could individually be drawn into OECD membership or EEC association. If they should then try to augment their status in this wider economic community, they might seek to reinforce their position by establishing closer economic ties with their East European neighbours and by trying to involve them in the common venture. A closer economic integration within Eastern Europe could thus evolve simultaneously with the all-European integrative process, without necessarily having to precede such development. The task of the joint economic association would be to define fundamental goals and to proceed to implement these through arrangements on tariff policy, transportation programmes, joint capital investment projects, and accords on at least temporary labour mobility, as well as through a partial accommodation on commodity pricing and marketing procedures.

The fundamental economic differences between the two political systems impose clearly recognizable lines of limitation on any multilateral economic association. But within the confines of these, there remains a considerable area of manoeuvrability. Eastern and Western Europe not only form one geographic unit and retain certain forms of cultural unity, but also display the highest degree of economic complementarity. The ruptured transportation and communication network is not beyond repair. The isolated, sporadic and restricted nature of bilateral agreements over the past few years in the area of tariff reduction and capital investments will have to be transformed into major and continuous programmes on a multilateral scale. The growing East European dependence on Western markets for the export, not only of agricultural products but also of a growing variety and volume of industrial goods, and their need of Western capital provide a potent inducement for wider accord. The East European needs, in turn, are complemented by labour shortages in Western Europe, a deficiency that could in some cases be met by facilitating the temporary westward migration of East European labour, along the German-Yugoslavian pattern of recent years. Or, more feasibly, it could be met by engaging the services of this labour force on its home territory through the medium of exporting capital to Eastern Europe to finance joint economic ventures.

In Western Europe the economic breakthrough from a protected national to an integrated international economic framework was not achieved by the perpetuation of traditional bilateral trade patterns but through a novel multilateral experiment; similarly a real economic breakthrough in relations with Eastern Europe would require the medium of a multilateral economic plan. Insofar as the execution of such a plan would also concern the economic interests of those West European countries which are not members of EEC and would, furthermore, touch upon consequential political and security matters which involve the United States and other Atlantic powers, the participation of the latter in the pre-proposal planning stage would seem essential.

The North Atlantic Alliance would not be directly involved in any of these activities, and any attempt to provide NATO with a more immediate responsibility and association with these matters might handicap the experiment. The attitude of the East European powers toward NATO is less likely to be marked by the goodwill and positive expectations that a multilateral economic organization might generate. Also, the U.S.S.R. would be less inclined to oppose the association of its allies with a European economic community than with an organization that had military overtones and gave the impression of a transfer of alliance allegiance.

The role of NATO in this economic process would be a more indirect one. In the first place, the Atlantic Alliance has the advantage of involving within one organization those powers which would directly participate in an expanded integrated European economic community and those which would not, even though the latter would still have an interest in the venture. Consultation and exchange of information within NATO could help bridge the gap between these two groupings of powers. Even more important, the continued security association of the two European groupings with their respective super-power, either through NATO or the Warsaw Pact, would be of principal assistance in the economic experiment, because it would give its participants a feeling of protection, and thus a greater willingness to accept changes during the risky and unpredictable first stages of the new programme. This would be of special interest to the East European powers whose continued affiliation with Moscow would act as a safeguard for the preservation of the basic political and social features of the established Communist régimes. It would be unrealistic to assume that the East European governments would voluntarily engage in an economic experiment that was clearly designed to threaten their existence. The safeguards of alliance membership would therefore be of assistance in soliciting a favourable response from Eastern Europe. The superpowers, too, are more likely to assent to the development of an all-European economic association if, at least during the initial phase, the continued existence of the established alliance systems could help persuade them that this particular form of economic development in Europe was not intended to threaten their basic interests in Europe, i.e., their continued access to the European economic bloc, the preservation of European peace and stability, and the maintenance of some of the principal features of the social order as it exists in Europe.

FORCE ADJUSTMENT IN EUROPE

Another area where the Alliance might be involved both directly and indirectly in the process of controlled or guided change is the balanced reduction of military forces from the European region. In the military sphere, even more than in the economic sector, the Alliance plays the role of providing a stabilizing and security mechanism that supports initiatives in the implementation of the *détente.*

Since the concern of the Alliance is with security and since arms control can be regarded as a security measure, the argument has often been advanced that NATO, which possesses a large military planning staff, would not be adequately discharging its tasks if it did not devote at least part of its energies and intelligence to the study and proposals on arms control and disengagement measures. Part of this failure must be attributed to the fact that the whole security concept of NATO's military organization has been geared to the task of establishing the maximum possible defence posture in terms of size and efficiency, and not to invent the means to reduce this. In addition, allied authorities may also argue that the Eighteen Nations Disarmament Conference or other organizations would provide a more proper forum for the discussion of arms control measures and force reduction proposals, and that participation by the Alliance would introduce additional problems, negative spill-over, duplication, and conflicting competence.

In the recent past attention has largely concentrated on the question of how to introduce mutual arms control measures in the European area. Various proposals have been advanced on this particular subject. Among these have been proposals for improved East-West crisis communication, for trading liaison officers who would act as observers and communication links, for the exchange of information on manoeuvres and troop movements, and the joint manning of radar screens as part of an air inspection system. All of these proposals have in common the aim to prevent war by accident or miscalculation. The two principal alliance systems could conceivably make proposals of this nature and, following agreement, provide the administrative framework to carry them into effect.

But when applied to present conditions, much of the original rationale for these marginal arms control agreements has become somewhat irrevelant. In the first place, the hope that one might be able to edge forward to some form of *détente* by agreement on these military terms has already been superseded by the prior emergence of such a *détente*, without any preceding arms control accommodation measures in the European area. Secondly, the fear of accidental war has become less acute because of technological improvements, such as the use of electronic locks to check against the unauthorized use of the widely distributed tactical nuclear weapons, and because of reciprocal actions by the super-powers, as for example the installation of the "hot line". Finally, the very existence of the strategic nuclear equilibrium has stabilized the entire situation to a degree where minor accidents or probing actions could be absorbed without forcing a major escalatory response. While the above-listed arms control measures still command some interest, they seem to have passed the stage of maximum yield which they may once have possessed.

The over-all strategic situation and the improved frame-

work of East-West political relations now make it possible
for NATO to direct itself to the more far-reaching question
of planning for a gradual and balanced reduction of forces
from the European area. At present we may already witness
the first stage in the process of force reductions, as the
gradually emerging East-West *détente* allows countries to
give priority to political and economic issues at the expense
of military considerations. In France General de Gaulle is
willing to gamble on a policy of greater national independence even at the risk of impairing the defence of France.
The recent decision to accept a modest reduction, or at any
rate a redeployment from home bases, of U.S. and British
forces in Germany demonstrates how foreign exchange and
budgetary considerations helped bring about a military decision of major importance. Economic considerations or
military preoccupations *vis-à-vis* China may prompt a similar reduction of Soviet troops from Eastern Europe in the
near future.

Under the political and strategic conditions which exist
in 1967 these steps seem natural, if not inevitable, and not
undesirable. What might be witnessed over the next few
years is a series of independent and modest steps that involve force reductions in Europe, where it will probably be
difficult to draw the line between the overlapping spheres of
unilateral and reciprocal behaviour. These steps will be
reciprocal insofar as their continuation would be contingent
on some measure of response from the other side. But they
would also be unilateral, as they would not follow from any
formally negotiated agreement. In fact, it might be undesirable during this initial and delicate phase of the experiment
to engage in formal negotiations, with all the risks of incurring negative feedback as the result of a deadlock. At the
outset, the daily pragmatic concern with meeting routine
economic and political demands might act as a safer and
more reliable agent of change than summit conferences and
the introduction of more ambitious blueprints.

The role of NATO in this process of force reduction is
likely to be a passive one. As in the case of an all-European

economic solution, changes of the *status quo* will be facilitated if allies may continue to count on a treaty of reinsurance to protect them against temporary imbalances and unpredictable and dangerous consequences that might follow from a major policy innovation. Neither the abolitionists, who want to see the earliest possible termination of the Alliance, nor NATO champions, who might want to involve the Alliance in proposals and negotiations for political change, are going to derive much comfort from this formula of rather passive Alliance behaviour.

A more active role might be reserved for the situation where a more advanced form of East-West *rapprochement* would make formal negotiations on troop reductions in Europe and a European political settlement a more realistic prospect than it is in the present context. Under those circumstances, NATO might conceivably serve to facilitate a final settlement by helping to adjust different allied positions to a common negotiable platform. Similarly, those powers most directly affected by a de-nuclearized status and by troop reductions might demand some form of compensation in the form of guarantees by the U.S. and other allies. Under those conditions the joint framework of a reformed Atlantic Alliance would serve as a more effective instrument of stability and would be politically more acceptable to the recipients than a series of bilateral guarantees and force redeployment arrangements.

Given all the problems which NATO encountered in creating a defence system in Western Europe, there now exists a natural reluctance to utilize the Alliance for the purpose of disbanding at least part of its military structure in order to fulfil far-reaching political aims. Even the recently announced reductions of British and U.S. forces in Germany, involving one British brigade and two U.S brigades and some hundred fighter planes, reflected a budgetary concern rather than a more fundamental calculation on NATO's political goals.

In contemplating military changes it is necessary that we retain the proper perspective of the principal aims for which NATO exists. This is of particular importance in a situation where the means are very complex and where the long-term ends are not realizable in the near future, with the result that means are frequently treated like final aims. The NATO machinery was set up with the immediate aim of preventing aggression in Europe. But it also served the more far-reaching goal of reaching a political settlement and of restoring normal political relations in Europe. The over-all strategic equilibrium and the partial East-West *détente* which have emerged now serve to uphold NATO's immediate security aim, thus making it desirable that the Alliance devote its means and capabilities to the realization of its more far-reaching political goals.

7
NATO in the Next Decade

Making predictions about the future of NATO is becoming an increasingly more arduous and risky task. The increase in East-West contacts and the greater decision-making latitude of the smaller allies have created a more mobile political situation in Europe than existed in the past. The result has been a proliferation of new variables that must be included in any analysis that deals with possible future trends and developments in the Alliance. This picture differs substantially from the static confrontation in Europe that prevailed during the Cold War when mobility was largely equated with a massive Soviet military advance rather than viewed in terms of political evolution. Consequently, there existed the tendency to treat the question of Soviet military intentions in Europe as the great unknown factor, while regarding as constant all other issues which affected Europe. The reverse applies now. In making calculations about future developments, the improbability of a large-scale Soviet aggression can be regarded as a constant factor, while all other aspects of Europe's political future represent relatively unknown quantities.

In addition to problems in prediction, it has become more difficult to evaluate NATO's level of performance. Former standards of behaviour and habits must be subjected to a critical reappraisal in order to determine their continuing utility under altered circumstances. In addition to such old criteria as NATO's military effectiveness, which can be measured somewhat more easily in terms of military hardware and by the size of forces, as well as by the *de facto* result of successful deterrence, we must now include new standards of judgement, as for example the role of the Alliance in facilitating a stable political transition in Europe. These two roles are not always complementary and, at least in the short run, the simultaneous pursuit of several goals might subject the Alliance to internal conflict.

The recent pattern of relations within and between the two major alliance systems has done much to dispel our former confidence in the belief that the political transformation of Europe would proceed as part of a carefully planned and centrally controlled process under the direction of closely knit military alliances or formally integrated communities. Even though the present mood about European security and the evolving relations between Eastern and Western Europe is one of growing, though cautious, optimism, analysts are becoming increasingly less inclined to link these developments to bold organizational reform proposals and idealized visions of a brave new Atlantic future, whether in terms of an Atlantic confederation or a geometrically balanced "two-pillar" system.

The concept of an Atlantic federal solution has never found a strong resonance in Europe. The Atlantic "federalists" have largely been recruited from the ranks of U.S. writers and politicians. This may partly be a reflection of the strong tradition of missionary idealism and the enthusiasm for bold new enterprises that characterizes much of American life and politics. A federal solution is also more likely to appeal to those who are advocating the formal abrogation of certain sovereign rights in the knowledge that most of these may be recovered on a *de facto* basis by virtue of the dominant role the United States would automatically play in an Atlantic confederation. Conversely, those allies who seek to preserve a degree of independence from the United States tend to express an intuitive preference for the well-tempered anarchy of the present pre-federal stage. In cultivating intimate ties with the United States, the West European powers were primarily concerned with military protection and not with the idea of political union or partnership. Now that the defence theme has become less central to European thinking, fear of domination by the United States has become a more important element in European policies.

The less ambitious idea of an equitably balanced Atlantic partnership, sometimes referred to by such labels as the "dumb-bell" concept or the "two-pillar" approach, which enjoyed great favour with the senior officials of the Kennedy Administration, has had a greater appeal to the European allies but has not been any more successful in actual practice. Since the early 1960's, when the "two-pillar" concept attracted considerable attention and, at least in the case of the United States, official support, there has been no visible breakthrough toward political unification in Western Europe despite progress in economic integration.[1] Thus the principal prerequisite for the "two-pillar" scheme is lacking.

Apart from their preoccupation with economic integration, the West European powers are also responding to the more fluid political situation gradually emerging in Europe and are consequently becoming more absorbed with building bridges to Eastern Europe. Attention to Atlantic

[1]It might even be said that the successful experiment of European economic integration, which was carried into effect by a group of nation states claiming full political sovereignty, has done much to restore the belief in the viability and constructive nature of politically sovereign nation states, a belief which had been severely shaken by two world wars. At present it is, therefore, more difficult to find popular acceptance for proposals that seek to replace the national community by a politically integrated international structure.

community affairs has accordingly diminished. U.S. involvement in Asia has had similar effects. Even the most complex government machinery has limits of available resources of time, energy, endurance, intelligence, and of imagination, for which the various regional involvements and functional preoccupations must compete. In the face of other absorbing issues, the concept of an Atlantic community gets a lower priority rating on either side of the Atlantic. As Karl Deutsch concludes from his recent survey of European elite opinions: "[t]he vision of a rich, multidimensioned and growing Atlantic Community has faded."[2]

In view of these observations, it might be more realistic to exclude the concept of an Atlantic, or even a West European, political superstructure from calculations about the course of events in that area during the decade to come. Political and military changes in Europe are likely to proceed in a zig-zag pattern of separate, though interdependent, actions and initiatives, without any high degree of central direction.

PROJECTED SITUATIONS: 1970 AND 1975

Any prediction about future trends in the Atlantic Alliance will have to rest on certain principal assumptions. Among these is the assumption that a "mega-war" will be avoided; that local conflict situations will be insulated and will not escalate to the level of a direct military confrontation between the two super-powers; and that the members of the two principal alliance systems will continue to enjoy uninterrupted economic growth.

In presenting the following charts on possible military developments in the European area during the next decade, no claim to predictive accuracy or special strategic insight is made. The reason for presenting a subject of such highly speculative nature in this particular form lies in the possible

[2] Karl Deutsch, "Integration and Arms Control in the European Political Environment", *American Political Science Review*, LX, No. 2 (June 1966), p. 360.

benefit we might derive from having a more specific framework for examining the interaction of the military, political, and economic factors with reference to East-West relations in Europe. It might also be of some assistance in exploring prospective areas of mobility and resistance in the process of political and military change in Europe.

Taking the situation in 1967, we are faced with approximately the following military build-up in the central area of Europe, which would be the most important target for military or political change.

Distribution of Principal Ground Forces in the Centre of Europe—1967

Nato Forces in West Germany	Warsaw Pact Forces in East Germany
6 U.S. divisions	20 Soviet divisions
12 West German divisions	6 East German divisions
3 British divisions	
2 French divisions	*Soviet Forces in Eastern Europe other than East Germany*[3]
1 Dutch division	
1 Belgian division	2 Soviet divisions in Poland
1 Canadian brigade	4 Soviet divisions in Hungary

The recent decision by Britain and the United States to reduce their forces in Germany is likely to produce a similar chain reaction in the behaviour of the other allies. The trend toward further force reductions seems to have been reinforced by the fact that the latest programme of the Bonn coalition government envisages considerable savings in its military budget over the next four years. Most likely, though not inevitably, the principal effect of this measure will be a decrease in the size of Germany's armed forces. One could hardly imagine that the smaller allies would re-

[3] The size of the forces of the other Warsaw Pact powers is both militarily and politically less relevant to the over-all development of the situation in Europe.

frain from imitating the pattern set by their principal partners. Finally, one would also have to take into consideration that the legal timetable date in the NATO Treaty may provide the occasion for a substantial revision in strategy, force levels, and the organizational framework of the Alliance after 1969.

By 1970 Germany might well have succeeded in establishing a more relaxed and business-like working atmosphere with most of the East European powers—in some cases also accompanied by diplomatic relations—somewhat along the pattern that now seems to be evolving in the relations between Bonn and Bucharest. The military situation in Europe in 1970 might approximate the following:

Distribution of Principal Ground Forces in the Centre of Europe—1970

NATO Forces in West Germany	Warsaw Pact Forces in East Germany
4 U.S. divisions	16-20 Soviet divisions
10 West German divisions	6 East German divisions
1 British division	*Soviet Forces in Eastern Europe other than East Germany*
1 French division	
	2 Soviet divisions in Poland
	2-4 Soviet divisions in Hungary

According to the 1970 estimates, the continued step-by-step reduction of the forces of the principal NATO allies and the total withdrawal of the troops of the smaller allies from Germany are treated as reasonably probable events. The chances that the Warsaw Pact powers would maintain a similar pace in the reduction of their forces in the central area of Europe are considerably lower. The Soviet Union has given no indication so far of its willingness to try to promote political relaxation by this particular strategy. Previous proposals by the Warsaw Pact members have preferred the formal approach of calling for the immediate abolition of the two alliance systems rather than the more pragmatic method of gradual force withdrawals that would be conducted under the auspices of the two alliances. Any withdrawal of Soviet troops from the territory of its Warsaw Pact allies during the next three years is likely to be minimal and would probably follow less from internal economic or allied pressures than from the desire to promote a disproportionately higher response on the side of the NATO powers.

But in the long run the combination of other military preoccupations, internal economic demands, and political pressures from its allies would make it increasingly difficult for the Soviet Union to leave its military posture in Eastern Europe unchanged.

Given the present rate of economic growth and conditions of political stability, the East European countries should make substantial progress in edging forward to the stage of mass-consumption societies within the next decade. As may be observed with the mass-consumption societies of North America and, more recently, of Western Europe, innovation is likely to be sought through high standards of managerial and technological efficiency rather than by the pursuit of a revolutionary programme. In the practical operation of their economies the East European powers might therefore be expected to demonstrate an increasing commitment to a pragmatic form of materialism instead of the more abstract materialism of Marxist doctrine. This, in turn, would enhance the bargaining position of those elite groups who derive their power from managerial and technological competence rather than from the manipulation of political symbols. Because of their pragmatic philosophy and orientation toward efficient performance, these new managerial elites may well demand greater freedom of choice and expression, as well as better access to information and to the material and cultural products from non-communist countries. The same groups might also be inclined to exert pressure in favour of reduced defence expenditures and force levels in order to stimulate economic growth and intra-European economic co-operation.

The rationale for taking the initiative in reducing some of the NATO forces in Europe lies in the fact that such action would generate pressures and inducements in the U.S.S.R. and Eastern Europe that might eventually spark similar military countermeasures and thus furnish the basis for a balanced process of force reductions.

These pressures might already within the next decade force the Soviet Union to engage in a partial withdrawal of its troops from the territory of its allies. At first the U.S.S.R. might be more inclined to restrict its policy of force adjustments to Hungary and Poland, especially as these two allies might exert pressure in this direction after improving their relations with West Germany, and to exclude the politically and militarily more vulnerable régime in East Germany from this process. But a moderate thinning out of Soviet forces from the D.D.R. before 1975 does not seem to lie entirely outside the realm of the possible.

In consideration of these factors one might envisage a military structure in Europe in 1975 somewhat along the following lines:

Distribution of Principal Ground Forces in the Centre of Europe—1975

NATO Forces in West Germany	Warsaw Pact Powers in East Germany
2 U.S. divisions 8 West German divisions 1 British brigade 1 French brigade	10-14 Soviet divisions 4 East German divisions *Soviet Forces in Eastern Europe other than East Germany* Only temporary visiting units during manoeuvres

According to the above projection, the trend toward a gradual withdrawal of "visiting" NATO forces from West Germany, which was already indicated in the estimates for the 1967-1970 period, is likely to continue until 1975, with the result that these forces would retain little more than symbolic significance. But the projections for 1975 differ substantially from the estimates for 1970, as they attach greater weight to the possibility that the Soviet Union would, by that time, have reacted to some of the same foreign and domestic pressures that originally motivated the NATO countries to embark on the process of force reductions. Soviet resistance to such pressures will naturally be strong, for the Soviet Union cannot but view with fundamental suspicion those efforts by NATO members that seek to entangle the East European powers in a web of closer relations with the West and that try to exert a moderating influence on the East European social order. But these forces of resistance will have to face increasingly stronger competition in the face of growing pressures from the camp of its own allies, because of shifting economic and military priorities for the Soviet Union and as a consequence of the overriding goal of avoiding a confrontation in Europe.

NEW TRENDS AND CHANGING HABITS IN THE ATLANTIC ALLIANCE

One might indicate other trends that are likely to affect the future behaviour of the Alliance, although it would be difficult to link these changes to any approximate timetable.

Gradual acceptance of the belief that conflict situations in Europe are more likely to arise from local instabilities rather than from massive premeditated aggression, as well as the reduction of force levels and the large-scale withdrawal of "visiting" forces, will tend to remove much of the original rationale for military integration in the Atlantic Alliance. In addition, the political arguments for integration would become less pressing with respect to Germany. The military and political problem of accommodating a large concentration of foreign troops on German territory, which the integration mechanism helped solve, would diminish once most of these forces had been removed. In future a more independently functioning German military establishment might cause less fear among its neighbours if Germany itself had made substantial military cuts, and if there would be a general improvement of relations between Germany and her Eastern neighbours. As the emphasis on integration is being reduced, the German government will come under increasing internal pressure to follow the example of its allies by creating a German general staff and by placing its forces under national command.

What will remain of NATO's integrated defence structure after 1975 will in all probability be smaller and less complex in character and more European in its staffing and management. Integration at that stage is likely to concentrate on the management of a joint air, and possibly also missile, defence system in Europe. Integration would also serve to maintain a co-operative link between Germany and those allies who had stationed forces on German territory or had earmarked air-mobile units for deployment on Europe's central front or flank areas in case of emergency.

The greater feeling of security among the members of NATO would tend to exert a centrifugal influence on their political behaviour both within and outside the Alliance. The kaleidoscopic pattern of relations within the Alliance is therefore bound to grow in complexity, with an increase in special bilateral relations or regional ties within the Atlantic framework. Those special relations which existed among the United States, Britain, and Canada have not been eliminated by the existence of NATO. Alliance membership merely seems to have added another dimension to these special ties. In certain instances, the existence of NATO has promoted the emergence of a new set of special relationships, as for example that which now exists between the United States and Germany, which to a large measure derives its basis from the presence of U.S. troops on German soil as part of the common NATO defence system. This, in turn, has provided for special relations between Germany and the United States in the sector of defence production and on a wider array of political questions.

Under improved security conditions some allies, especially those on the NATO flanks, might be prompted to duplicate the recent French example of partial disengagement from allied activities. Internal conflict situations, such as the Cyprus issue, might induce some members to cultivate friendly bilateral relations with Moscow and to sever their NATO association altogether.

Conditions thus do not seem to favour an expansion in the range of commitments or an increase in the number of NATO allies. If the present trend toward greater pluralism in the interests of the NATO allies continues, then the insistence on universal consensus on all major issues facing the Alliance would result in a situation where common action and agreement would be reduced to the lowest common denominator. But to take the reverse approach, and to aim for special engagements and additional responsibilities among a selective group of allies who display a higher level of consensus, might exert a divisive impact on the Alliance as a whole.

NATO is thus confronted with the dilemma of either choosing to maintain greater cohesion under selective groupings or of insisting on universal representation, at the cost of lower homogeneity and possible paralysis. The establishment of a selective nuclear planning group and the determined effort of the rest of the Alliance to organize the defence of Europe largely without French participation give the impression that the present trend in NATO does, indeed, lead to higher fragmentation and various special working groups rather than toward greater universality. The crystallization of separate groupings within the Alliance would duplicate the emergence of the "Inner Six" from the more universal but less cohesive European Council, or NATO's own beginning, when a regional group of states considered the security benefits of the United Nations inadequate and therefore decided to assume more explicit military commitments. In neither case did the members of the new selective commitment group leave the more universal parent organization, nor was the operation of the latter noticeably impaired by this development.

In future more allies might be persuaded to opt for an

absolute minimum of Alliance entanglements by confining their role to formal membership in the Alliance, and to participate in the political activities of the NATO Council. Despite this trend, some members, because of special security needs or the desire to have a better opportunity to influence the policy of the United States or other allies, would want to continue to participate in the integrated military defence system in Europe, at least until the present build-up of military forces in the European area had been substantially modified.

Still fewer allies might be willing to assume an even more active role by accepting a more direct association with nuclear weapons and policy than what they already derive from membership in an alliance that relies on nuclear deterrence. Nuclear association might take the form of accepting tactical nuclear weapons under a "dual-key" control system, or it might lead to the development of a jointly owned and managed Atlantic nuclear force, as was reflected in the MLF scheme. More likely, however, it would take the form of participation in NATO's newly formed nuclear planning group.

The restrictive membership on such a nuclear committee is partly determined by the dictates of efficient nuclear management, and partly by the unwillingness of some allies to undertake any further commitments under NATO. The latter attitude may be attributed to reluctance to assume a more intimate nuclear association, as is largely the case with the Scandinavian members, or, as in the case of France, it may stem from the unwillingness to sacrifice the reality, or semblance of, an independent nuclear defence posture.

THE "POLITIZATION" OF NATO

From the above-listed examples one gets the general impression that the Alliance will become somewhat more "demilitarized" in its operations and increasingly political in its orientation. Even though its primary concern will continue to be with military matters, the existence of a highly mobile political situation, superimposed on a less flexible strategic foundation, will necessitate a greater political orientation in the role of the Alliance. This would be of special importance with respect to those shadow areas of overlapping military and political involvement, as for example the creation of a system of crisis management, the signing of a non-proliferation treaty, and the mutual reduction of forces in the European area. The military problems that will confront the Alliance in future will be more directly dominated by the political aims and priorities of its members than was the case in the past. It would therefore seem desirable that NATO address itself to making the necessary functional and organizational adaptations in order to cope with this trend.

The creation of the NATO nuclear planning group may be regarded as a step in this direction, for the management of nuclear affairs comprises not only questions of military strategy but also more general issues of foreign policy and economics.

The need to lay the groundwork for an allied system of crisis management and crisis avoidance, both of which involve political and psychological elements in addition to purely military factors, is closely connected with the issue of nuclear planning and management. As at present constituted, the military structure and political organization of the Alliance is not fully geared to the task of crisis management. NATO's integrated defence system in Europe concentrates too much on the actual use of force following the outbreak of hostilities. Not enough emphasis is given to the planned direction of those composite military, political, and psychological factors that underlie a crisis and which, if used diligently, might prevent a crisis from escalating to the stage of physical violence. The previous concentration on the ability to launch a massive military response in the event of hostilities in Europe was the correct approach for the Alliance at a time when the principal threat seemed to be that of a full-scale premeditated attack by the Soviet Union. However, in future the danger will increasingly lie with local instabilities and conflict situations in Europe that would have to be countered by the adroit management of the related military and political factors rather than by massive military intervention.

The North Atlantic Council alone cannot properly carry out this managerial task. Because of its size and the nature of its other routine functions it is not very suitable for the kind of intimate political and military staff work that would be required in order to lay the ground rules for the management of crisis situations.

The role of contingency planning for crisis situations might be delegated to a group of experts. But given the lack of political integration in the Alliance, only a directorate of the heads of government of those allies most closely involved with a particular crisis would be capable of making the more far-reaching decisions during a crisis situation. As is true for the nuclear control issue, so also with the question of crisis management there can be no absolute but only a relative guarantee that the final response in a crisis would be in accordance with preceding plans and accords. But the probability of common agreement would be enhanced by a technically improved communications system, a kind of network of "hot lines" between allied heads of government, and secondly, by the creation of a set of contingency plans.

The aim of contingency planning is to establish general guiding principles for action in a crisis situation, to take different allied views into consideration and to reconcile these, if at all possible. "Contingency planning", as defined by Alastair Buchan,

> is not, as it is sometimes represented, the drawing up of firm plans to meet an indefinite variety of hypotheses about the forms that the threat to a particular area could take, which can be pulled out of a card index when the adversary pushes a particular button, and immediately translated into action. It is much more a question of deciding what is the general scope of the reaction which it is realistic to contemplate, what are the limitations, what preparatory action is necessary, what courses of

action must be ruled out, and often of testing these judgements by extensive and prolonged war games.[4]

To aim for full agreement in advance on every conceivable step that might be taken in a crisis situation would be unrealistic in view of the fact that even the most imaginative plan could not hope to duplicate all the intricate details and imponderables of a specific situation in reality. Furthermore, even if nations were fully bent on abiding by a pre-arranged strategy, it cannot be predicted that their actual reaction at a time of extreme tension would correspond exactly to the behaviour envisaged in the more detached atmosphere of a contingency planning session.

NATO's nuclear planning group might develop into a forum for the management of crisis situations that involve the direct threat, or actual use, of nuclear weapons. Since under present conditions a crisis in Europe is more likely to occur as the result of local instabilities, probing actions, and political pressures than in the form of a massive confrontation, one can make a good argument in favour of establishing contingency planning and crisis management organizations on the basis of regional groups.[5] The activities of these separate regional groupings would have to be closely co-ordinated. Co-ordination would be assisted by the overlapping membership in different groups and by the central role of the NATO Council.

These measures would not constitute any new commitments or an intensification of the over-all activities under the auspices of NATO, which would be quite contrary to the present trend. But they would represent some form of adjustment to the more fluid military and political situation that is now emerging in Europe.

[4] Alastair Buchan, *Crisis Management: The New Diplomacy* (Atlantic Institute, Atlantic Papers, NATO Papers, II, 1966), p. 42.

[5] Buchan (*ibid.*, p. 49) suggests a northern group, consisting of the U.S., Britain, Denmark, Norway, and Germany; a southern group, composed of the U.S., Italy, Greece, Turkey, Portugal, Britain, and France, if the latter should agree to this more active form of participation; and a central group, including the U.S., Britain, Germany, Canada, Holland, Belgium, and France.

In addition to the nuclear planning group and to the regional planning organizations, it might also be practical to make similar arrangements on an *ad hoc* basis in order to handle those problems that more directly affect the particular commitments and interests of certain allies but are of less immediate concern to the rest of the Alliance. The system of contingency planning that was improvised during the Berlin crisis and involved those allies with direct interests and commitments in Berlin—in this particular case, the U.S., Britain, France, and Germany—could serve as a model for an *ad hoc* type of crisis management organization.

Still another response to the increased "politization" of NATO affairs would be the creation of an intimate and permanent high-level policy planning staff, a kind of multilateralized version of the policy planning staffs that already exist in the Foreign Offices of several of the major allies. Political consultation, which already operates on the level of the NATO Council and the Political Advisers Committee, represents one facet of the process of political planning. These two bodies perform the necessary and valuable task of providing a routine scanning job on a wide range of subjects of current concern. But the enormous dimensions of the task and the large size of the plenary NATO forum detract from the opportunity to undertake a systematic study and rigorous analysis of certain specific and far-reaching political objectives. The role of the NATO Council may be compared to that of a hospital emergency ward. Necessary as the hospital emergency room is, it is not a very suitable place for the conduct of medical research. The Council's preoccupation with administering to current needs and demands detracts from the systematic study and voluntary introduction of new and complex political issues.

The only existing NATO organization that now approximates the functions of such a policy planning staff is the Atlantic Policy Advisory Group. But this particular body meets semi-annually and then only for a few days. What is required instead, in the first place, is a more permanent planning group, and secondly, one that consists of persons whose authority and competence would be recognized not only in their home country but also among the other allies. In setting up such a planning staff one would to a certain extent recreate on a permanent basis the former temporary committee of "Three Wise Men". Such a permanent planning group would supplement rather than replace the political functions of the other NATO bodies or of member-governments. According to one proposal, this planning group is to be given the equivalent political functions that, in the economic sphere, are now being exercised by the European Economic Commission, by virtue of its authority to formulate proposals on goals and policies, while leaving it to the member-governments to determine the practical means of implementation.[6] But given the present state of integration in the Atlantic region and the growth of pluralism in allied behaviour, there exists little indication that member-governments would be willing to abdicate to an international planning body any right of political proposal or individual initiative. To invoke the example of the EEC Commission may not be entirely relevant, for not only do economic matters provide a better subject for planning than the less tangible political and security questions, but the EEC Commission also operates in a milieu of basic consensus on fundamental goals. The role of the Commission, given the existence of a blueprint or cook-book of procedures, is one of finding the proper means of making this mandate operational. There exists at present no comparable concrete prescription for the political future of the North Atlantic region. In its absence, the role of such a Commission would not be one of implementing an existing plan but one of creating such a plan and of soliciting political consensus for it. A task of such far-reaching dimensions would exceed both the capabilities and the mandate that migh be given to a body of technocratic experts.

[6] Livingston Hartley, "Atlantic Commission of 'Wise Men' ", *Atlantic Community Quarterly*, Vol. II, No. 4 (Winter 1964-65), pp. 558-62.

CONCLUSIONS

In viewing the North Atlantic Alliance from a broader historical perspective, one can clearly distinguish between its initial growing phase, the period of implementation, and the period of reduction. The innovation phase, which may be said to have lasted until the admission of Germany, was characterized by geographic expansion and by bold new enterprises, such as the creation of a system of integrated defence in Europe and the establishment of an organization for permanent political consultation. The years between 1955 and 1962 may be regarded as a period of implementation and perfection of existing allied organizations, practices, and fighting power. At present, with the emergence of a strategic equilibrium between the super-powers and of a partial East-West *détente*, NATO seems to be engaged in a process of reduction. So far this has involved the French decision to withdraw from the integrated system of defence, the dissolution of such Alliance organizations as the Standing Group, the announced reduction of U.S. and British forces in Germany, and the cancellation of such ambitious projects as the MLF. All of these far-reaching measures have been taken within little more than a year. In line with this process of reduction, one should anticipate more military cuts, further abolitions of existing NATO structures, a simplification of the integrated defence system, and possibly even a complete withdrawal from the Alliance by some members.

Despite these changes, the basic rationale for the Alliance has remained constant. Then as now, NATO exists in order to counteract the effects of the military and political division of Europe and the forceful penetration of Soviet influence right into the heart of Europe. There would be no need, and little possibility, of retaining a formal alliance between North America and Western Europe once this internal European schism had been overcome. But it is equally improbable that the West European powers would voluntarily sacrifice an organization that was designed to counteract the effects of this division, as long as it continued to exist in its basic elements.

By subscribing to the above argument one may conclude that despite outside pressures and internal discontent, the Atlantic Alliance, in its concept and basic form though not necessarily in its present structure, will continue to exist during the next decade. Those who advocate the immediate dissolution of NATO in order to accelerate the rate of political change in Europe are, in the words of Britain's Foreign Minister, George Brown, "putting the military cart before the political horse"[7] for the abolition of alliances does not by itself get rid of the amalgamation of military forces in Europe. A fundamental revision of the military situation in Europe would largely depend on a preceding political settlement. But without such a settlement the dissolution of the system of existing alliances in Europe would, somewhat reminiscent of the situation that prevailed before World War II, leave the full array of separate national armies without an international regulatory infrastructure.

A summary decision to dismantle the system of alliances in Europe, a sort of bilateral scrapping agreement, would run the risk of jeopardizing the security and stability in that area. It would be a more proper procedure to try to minimize such risks by adopting a series of preceding measures and preliminary agreements, all of which would still be under the protective cover of the existing framework of alliances. Initially the focus would fall on the gradual reduction of military forces. These would be undertaken separately by the different allies but would aim for some degree of balance between the two sides.

If such unilateral measures should have helped improve the climate of East-West relations in Europe as well as create a desire for new approaches, a conference, or series of conferences, on European security might be held with a view to reaching agreement on the following slate of issues:

[7] George Brown, "East-West Relations and the European Problem", *NATO Letter* (February 1967), p. 4.

1) Agreement on a schedule for military reductions in the central area of Europe in order to establish a somewhat more formalized process of balanced force reductions than exists under conditions of purely unilateral measures;

2) Acceptance of non-nuclear status by all continental European powers with the exception of France and the U.S.S.R.;

3) Elimination of tactical nuclear weapons under "two-key" or "multiple-key" control system from the inventory of all the European powers who accept non-nuclear status.

Preliminary security agreements of this kind would not eliminate the system of alliances. But eventually they might pave the way for a more fundamental political settlement in Europe that would make the dissolution of NATO and the Warsaw Pact possible. The following would be some of the key features of such a security arrangement and political settlement in Europe:

1) German recognition of the Oder-Neisse line or of a somewhat similar German-Polish boundary with a few minor rectifications in favour of Germany;

2) Formal recognition by all signatories to this European political and security treaty, whether they be European or non-European powers, of the agreed territorial status in Europe;

3) Settlement of the German problem, either by agreeing on a strategy of gradual reunification at the time of the agreement, or by stipulating a future date when East and West Germany would be free to negotiate such a union or desired status of association without outside interference;

4) Agreement to withdraw, within a specified period of time, all "visiting" allied forces from German territory and the soil of the other NATO or Warsaw Pact powers in Europe;

5) Agreement on the non-nuclear status of Germany (or the two Germanies) and a ceiling on the conventional force levels of Germany (or the two Germanies), at least for a specified period of time, in return for international guarantees by all signatory powers;

6) Non-aggression pacts between the former members

of NATO on the one hand, and of the Warsaw Pact on the other.[8]

7) Dissolution of NATO and the Warsaw Pact.

Such scenarios of eventual political and security arrangements should not blind us to the fact that we have, at best, reached the first phase of the long process of *détente*-building in Europe.

If NATO were to be disbanded during this early phase of *détente*-building, we would lose the only organized forum that now exists for common action, consultation, and communication in the event of a renewed Berlin crisis or similar emergency situations in Europe.[9] While NATO cannot guarantee Germany's non-nuclear status is perpetuity, it does at present serve to dissuade Germany from creating an independent nuclear force, at a time when the incentive for nuclear status might be higher and its destabilizing effects on the European political situation greater than might be the case in future.

A precipitate dissolution of the Alliance might bring with it a resurgent feeling of insecurity in Europe. This would not serve as a favourable climate for military reductions. Also, without the collective alliance system there would be a lack of concerted response to unilateral measures such as a partial withdrawal of Soviet troops from East Germany. Some West European allies might react in the same fashion, but their separate measures would not have the same effect as a general co-ordinated response by the majority of NATO members.

We have learned from past events that the existence of their respective alliance involvements in Europe does not

[8] The value of such non-aggression treaties in the nuclear age is psychological rather than military, for it officially documents the willingness of the members of two previously hostile coalitions to change the nature of their relations.

[9] A new Berlin crisis would not necessarily have to be instigated by the Soviet Union. A more independent and self-assertive East German régime might start it by such actions as sending armed units into West Berlin in pursuit of East German refugees.

prevent the super-powers from establishing a bilateral dialogue. Without these alliance affiliations the super-powers could act more independently and would not be under the same compulsion to attune their dialogue to the wishes and reservations of other powers. The alliance system, therefore, has the effect of giving a more universal acceptability to bilateral accords between the super-powers. The nuclear non-proliferation treaty might serve as a case in point. The present negotiations concerning this particular treaty are as much concerned with establishing super-power consensus as with broadening the base of its acceptability to other powers.

During the past decade, the predominant sense of insecurity served to impose certain restraints and controls on the foreign policy of the European powers. The growing feeling of security and optimism will, in the decade ahead, lead to a more vigorous assertion of separate national interests and points of view. This in itself might develop into a source of renewed instability in Europe. In anticipating such a trend it may be wise to preserve certain countermeasures against possible excesses by cultivating those institutions and practices that could provide some degree of international communication, co-operation, multilaterality, and restraint. The North Atlantic Alliance has been, and could continue to be, an institution of this kind. Because the Alliance relies on voluntary co-operation rather than on more ambitious forms of supranationalism, its role over the next few years should prove to be compatible with the new European trend toward greater decentralization in political initiative and decision-making.

Much of the argument in favour of continuing the Alliance on a broader Atlantic foundation rather than on the basis of a purely regional European grouping would cease to be valid following the breakdown of the present division of Europe and the emergence of a new political order in Europe. The liquidation of NATO under those conditions, but not under present circumstances, could then be regarded as the natural and successful completion of its mission.